BELIZE
TRAVEL GUIDE 2024

Explore the Great Blue Hole, Barrier Reef, Xunantunich Ruins, Ambergris Caye, and Local Culture

SETH HICKSON

Copyright © Seth Hickson, 2024

All rights reserved. No part of this publication may be reproduced, distributed, or transmitted in any form or by any means, including photocopying, recording, or other electronic or mechanical methods, without the prior written permission of the publisher, except in the case of brief quotations embodied in critical reviews and certain other non-commercial uses permitted by copyright law.

TABLE OF CONTENTS

1. Introduction to Belize 9
   1.1 Overview of Belize 9
   1.2 Why Visit Belize 10
   1.3 A Brief History of Belize 12
   1.4 Cultural Overview and Diversity 14
2. Planning Your Trip 18
   2.1 Best time to visit..18
   2.2 Entrance Requirements and Visa Information 23
   2.3 Currency and Money Matters..............................31
   2.4 Language and Communication 39
   2.5 Health and Safety Tips..55
3. Getting to Belize..69
   3.1 Airports & Airlines..69
   3.2 Land Border Crossings 74
   3.3 Transportation in Belize 79
4. Accommodations 89
   4.1 Hotel and Resort..89
   4.2 Budget Accommodation 95
   4.3 Unique Stays.. 100
5. Exploring Belize 110
   5.1 Popular Destinations.. 110

5.2 Must-See Attractions 140
5.3 Outdoor Activities 144
6. Cultural Experiences 149
6.1 Local Culinary and Dining 149
6.2 Traditional Festivities and Events 156
6.3 Indigenous Culture and Communities 163
Wildlife and Nature 172
7.1 The Belize Barrier Reef 173
7.2 National Parks & Reserves 176
7.3 Bird Watching and Wildlife Sanctuaries 183
8. Practical Tips for Travelers 188
8.1 Packing Essentials 188
8.2 Local Etiquette and Customs 193
8.3 Internet & Communication 198
8.4 Emergency Contacts 204
8.5 LGBTQ+ Travel Tips 209
Sustainable and Responsible Tourism 213
9.1 Ecotourism Initiatives 213
9.2 Conservation Projects 216
9.3 Responsible Travel Tips 219
Additional Tips and Resources 227
10.1 Official Tourist Websites 227

10. 2 Travel Apps 229
10.3 Itinerary suggestions 231
10.4 FAQs 238

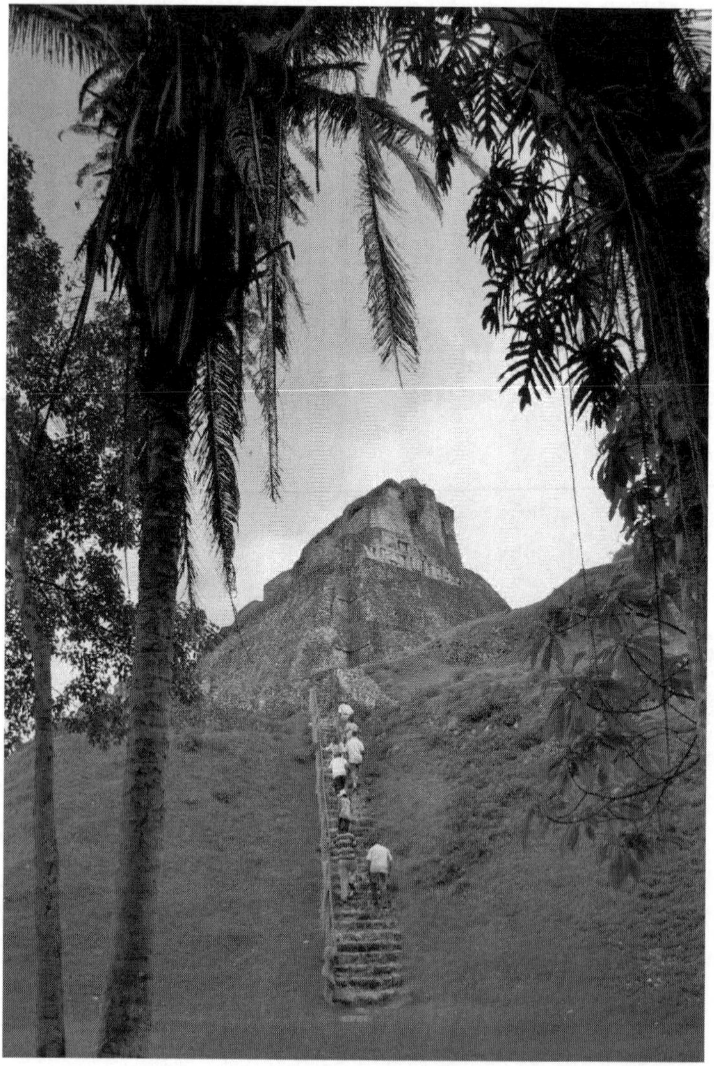

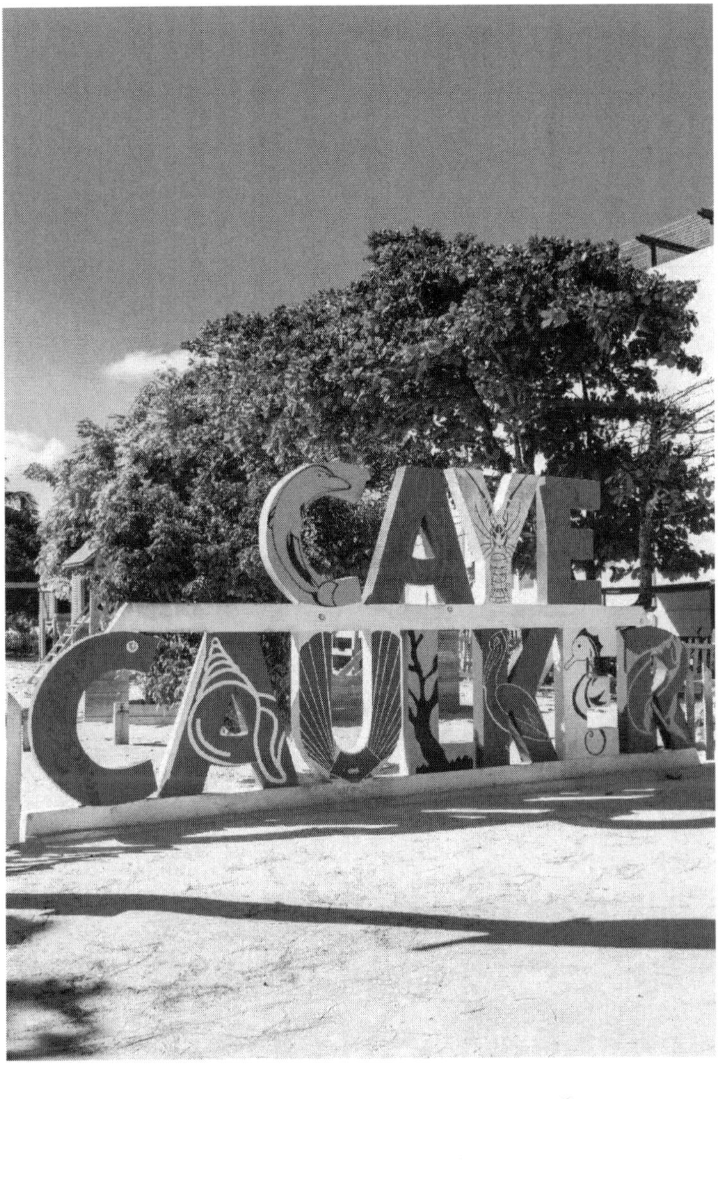
CAYE
CAULKER

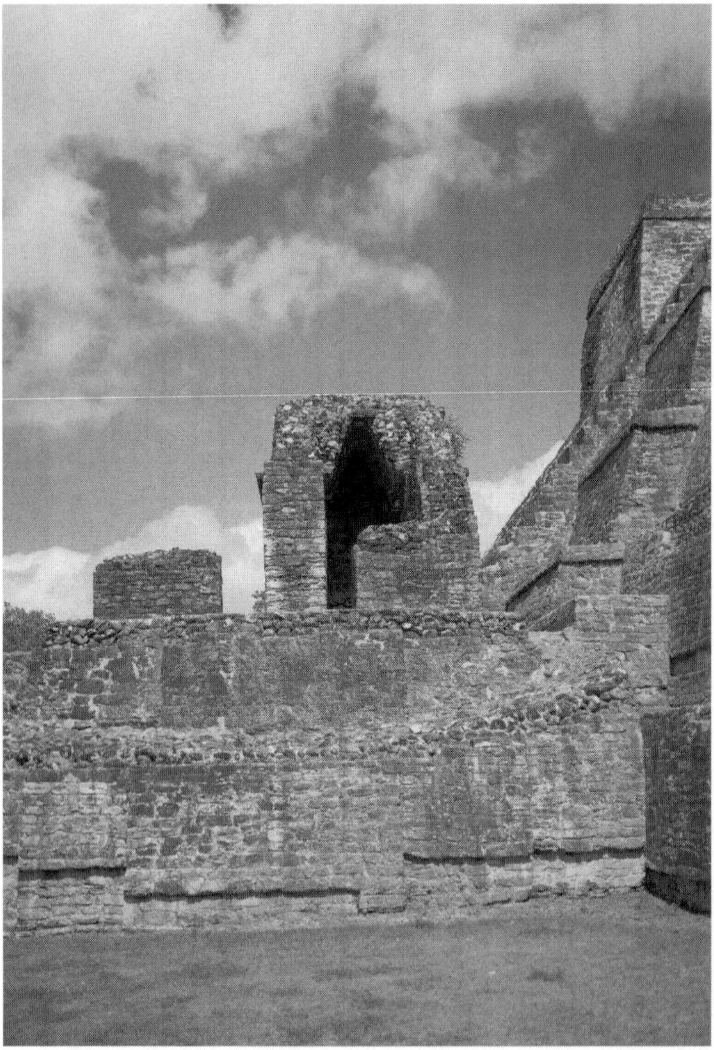

8

1. Introduction to Belize

1.1 Overview of Belize

Belize, a small republic on Central America's northeastern coast, borders to the north, Guatemala to the west and south, and the Caribbean Sea to the east. Belize has a physical area of around 22,970 square kilometers (8,867 square miles), making it one of the most ecologically diverse countries in the region. Its population of around 400,000 is made up of a varied mix of nations, including Mestizo, Creole, Maya, Garifuna, and others, all of which contribute to the country's particular cultural history.

Belize's geography is marked by stunning natural surroundings, ranging from lush rainforests and steep terrain in the west to clear beaches and the world-renowned Belize Barrier Reef in the east. The country's official language is English, making it an ideal location for English-speaking travelers, but Spanish, Creole, and various Mayan languages are also widely spoken.

The capital, Belmopan, is located inland, whereas Belize City, the largest metropolitan zone, serves as the primary business hub and gateway for many visitors. Belize's political system is a parliamentary democracy, and the country remains a Commonwealth member.

1.2 Why Visit Belize

Belize offers a unique blend of natural beauty, cultural variety, and adventure, making it an appealing destination for a wide range of visitors. Here are some compelling reasons to visit Belize:

Natural Wonders

Belize is home to the Belize Barrier Reef, the world's second-largest coral reef system, which provides unparalleled opportunities for snorkeling and diving. The Great Blue Hole, a massive underwater sinkhole, attracts divers from all over the world. Inland, the country boasts gorgeous forests, cascading waterfalls, and vast cave systems like the Actun Tunichil Muknal (ATM) Cave, which allow for thrilling experiences.

Rich Cultural Heritage

Belize's diverse cultural environment includes the ancient Maya culture, which has outstanding archeological sites such as Caracol, Xunantunich, and Lamanai. The Garifuna people are known for their vibrant music, dance, and cuisine, and Mestizo, Creole, and Mennonite groups, all contribute unique tastes to the cultural tapestry.

Adventure Activities

Belize is an adventurer's paradise, with zip-lining above jungle canopy, kayaking along peaceful rivers, and visits to ancient caverns. Wildlife reserves, like the Cockscomb Basin Wildlife Sanctuary, offer opportunities to observe uncommon birds and animals, including jaguars.

Ecotourism and Sustainability

Belize is strongly committed to conservation and sustainable tourism. Many eco-lodges and resorts emphasize environmental stewardship by providing eco-friendly guestrooms and activities that contribute to the preservation of natural habitats.

Relaxation & Wellness

Belize's beautiful islands, or "cayes," provide peaceful places to rest. Ambergris Caye and Caye Caulker provide gorgeous beaches, crystal-clear waters, and luxurious spas for a rejuvenating getaway.

1.3 A Brief History of Belize

The Pre-Columbian Era

Belize's history dates back thousands of years, with the ancient Maya civilization being one of the oldest and most powerful cultures in the region. The Maya established prosperous city-states, engaged in large commerce networks, and created great architectural marvels like temples, pyramids, and palaces. Sites such as Caracol, Lamanai, and Xunantunich provide witness to their tremendous culture, which thrived between 250 and 900 AD.

Colonial Period

In the 16th century, Spanish explorers arrived in the region, but they were met with resistance by the Maya who struggled to establish a presence. By the 17th century, British settlers were drawn to the region's valuable hardwood resources and began to establish logging camps along the coast. These residents, known as Baymen, frequently clashed with Spanish forces for control of the territory.

The Battle of St. George's Caye in 1798 was a watershed moment, with the Baymen successfully repelling a Spanish attack, and securing British control of the region. The town, formerly known as British Honduras, became a British colony in 1862.

Independence and Modern Era

The route to independence began in the mid-twentieth century when Belizeans advocated for greater self-government. British Honduras gained independence in

1964, and the country's name was officially changed to Belize in 1973. On September 21, 1981, Belize achieved full independence, but Guatemala retained territorial claims over the country.

Today, Belize is a stable and democratic country, known for its peaceful transition to independence and efforts to preserve its diverse cultural traditions and natural environment.

1.4 Cultural Overview and Diversity

Belize's cultural diversity is one of its most defining features, shaped by the influences of its many ethnic groups, each contributing to the country's cultural fabric.

The Maya

The Maya are Belize's indigenous people, with a history spanning more than 3,000 years. Belize now has three different Maya tribes: the Yucatec, Mopan, and Q'eqchi'. They keep their traditional customs, dialects, and rituals alive, and travelers may learn about Maya culture by visiting community centers, festivals, and archaeological sites.

The Garifuna

The Garifuna people, sprung from African and indigenous Carib and Arawak people, have a distinct culture known for vibrant music, dance, and storytelling. UNESCO has identified the Garifuna language as a Masterpiece of the Oral and Intangible Heritage of Humanity, and it is widely spoken in coastal villages such as Dangriga and Hopkins.

The Mestizo

The majority of Belize's population is made up of Mestizos, who are of mixed Spanish and indigenous heritage. Their influence is particularly strong in the northern and western regions, where Spanish is the major language. Mestizo culture is distinguished by a blend of Spanish and indigenous cultures, as seen by their cuisine, music, and festivals.

The Creole

Belizean Creoles, the offspring of African slaves and British colonizers, are mostly found in Belize City and surrounding areas. Creole culture is an important component of Belizean identity, and the Creole language (Kriol) is widely spoken. Creole cuisine, known for its savory and powerful dishes, is a symbol of Belizean culinary history.

The Mennonites

Mennonites, primarily of German and Dutch descent, migrated to Belize in the twentieth century and established agricultural settlements. They are known for their traditional lifestyle, agricultural skills, and distinctive dress. Mennonites make tremendous contributions to the Belizean economy, particularly in agriculture and dairy production.

Other Ethnic Groups

Minor ethnic groups in Belize include East Indians, Chinese, Lebanese, and expats from North America and Europe, all of whom contribute to the country's multicultural fabric.

Festivals and Celebrations

Belizeans celebrate their cultural diversity via various festivals and activities. Key events include Garifuna Settlement Day on November 19th, which commemorates the arrival of the Garifuna people, and Belize's Independence Day on September 21st, which features parades, music, and fireworks. The yearly Lobster Festivals in San Pedro, Placencia, and Caye Caulker are also popular, marking the lobster season with food, music, and festivities.

In summary, Belize's cultural diversity, rich history, and commitment to preserving its natural beauty make it a unique and appealing destination. Whether you're drawn to the ancient Maya ruins, the colorful customs of the Garifuna, or the stunning landscape of the Belize Barrier Reef, Belize has something for every traveler.

2. Planning Your Trip

2.1 Best time to visit

2.1.1 Climate and Weather Patterns

Belize has a tropical climate characterized by distinct wet and dry seasons. Understanding these weather trends is critical for planning your vacation and ensuring you have the best possible experience.

Dry Season: (Late November to Mid-April)

The dry season is often regarded as the best time to visit Belize. During this period, the weather is mostly bright, with no rain and temperatures ranging from 70°F (21°C) to 85°F (29°C). The dry season is also recognized as the peak season for tourism, with visitors gathering to enjoy the ideal weather conditions.

Key features of the dry season include:

- **Clear skies and sunshine** are ideal for outdoor activities including beach vacations, snorkeling, diving, and exploring archaeological sites.

- **Cooler Evenings:** Especially in the interior regions and at higher elevations, temperatures can drop to around 60°F (15°C) at night.

- **Higher pricing and crowds:** Because of the popularity of this season, hotel and tour rates tend to rise, and attractions may get congested. Early appointments are recommended.

Wet Season (middle of April until late November)

The rainy season, also known as the low season, has more rainfall, greater humidity, and warmer temperatures ranging from 75°F (24°C) to 95°F (35°C). While this may deter some visitors, the rainy season has its unique benefits.

Key features of the rainy season include:

- **Rain Showers:** Rain frequently falls in quick, forceful bursts, particularly in the afternoon or evening, leaving the mornings and early afternoons mostly dry. This strategy may still allow for plenty of outside activities.

- **Lush Landscapes:** The increased rainfall transforms the countryside into a vibrant, verdant paradise ideal for nature lovers and photographers.

- **Lower Prices and Fewer Crowds:** With fewer tourists, you could have a more relaxed and uncomplicated experience. Accommodation and travel costs are typically lower, and special deals and discounts are available regularly.

- **Hurricane Risk:** The wet season corresponds with the Atlantic hurricane season, which lasts from June to November. While hurricanes do not frequently strike Belize, it is critical to stay informed about weather conditions and have travel insurance that covers unanticipated problems.

2.1.2 Seasonal Events and Festivals

Belize's cultural calendar is filled with intriguing events and festivals all year. Timing your visit to coincide with these festivities may provide a deeper understanding of Belizean culture and traditions.

Dry Season Events and Festivals

- **Garifuna Settlement Day (November 19):** This event, held in coastal villages such as Dangriga, Hopkins, and Punta Gorda, commemorates the arrival of the Garifuna people in 1802. The activities include traditional drumming, dancing, parades, and cultural reenactments.

- **Christmas and New Year's Celebrations (December):** Belizean Christmas traditions include British and Caribbean influences, such as festive lighting, parades, and special church services. New Year's Eve celebrations and fireworks are popular in major cities and tourist locations.

- **Belize Carnival (September):** While the rainy season is technically over, this vibrant carnival marks the start of the Independence Day celebrations. It features colorful costumes, lively music, and street parades across Belize City.

- **Easter Festivities (March/April):** Easter is a significant celebration in Belize, with church processions, horse races, and beach parties, especially in San Pedro and Placencia.

Wet Season Events and Festivals

- **Lobster Festivals (June/July):** Held in San Pedro, Placencia, and Caye Caulker, these festivals commemorate the start of lobster season with culinary activities, live music, and contests. It's the ideal time to indulge in fresh lobster feasts.

- **Benque Viejo Del Carmen Fiesta (July):** This fiesta, held near the Guatemalan border, honors Our Lady of Mount Carmel, the town's patron saint. The activities include parades, music, dancing performances, and a fair.

- **Mango celebration (June):** Held in Hopkins, this event celebrates the mango harvest with food vendors, cooking contests, and cultural performances that highlight the diversity of this tropical fruit.

- **St. George's Caye Day (September 10):** This national holiday commemorates the 1798 Battle of St. George's Caye, during which the Baymen battled Spanish invaders. Parades, regattas, and historical reenactments are among the events held to celebrate.

- **Belize Independence Day (September 21):** This day commemorates Belize's independence from Britain in 1981, with patriotic parades, fireworks, cultural performances, and a variety of community events around the country.

2.2 Entrance Requirements and Visa Information

2.2.1 Tourist visas

Tourists visiting Belize normally require a valid passport. Visa requirements differ depending on the traveler's nationality and the length of their stay. The following are the key aspects of Belize tourist visas.

Visa-Exempt Countries

Citizens of several countries, including the United States, Canada, European Union member states, the United Kingdom, Australia, New Zealand, and many Caribbean and Central American countries, are not required to get a visa to visit Belize for stays of up to thirty days. Travelers from these countries must bring:

- A valid passport with at least six months remaining validity from the date of entrance.

- A return or onward ticket

- Proof of sufficient funds for the duration of the stay (often a bank statement or proof of lodging).

Visa-Required Countries

Citizens from countries not on the visa-exempt list must apply for a tourist visa before entering Belize. The application method consists of the following steps:

Application Form: Fill out the visa application form, which may be obtained at the nearest Belizean embassy or consulate or downloaded from their official website.

Supporting Documents: Submit the completed application form, together with the following documents:

- A valid passport with at least six months of validity remaining.

- A passport-size photo

- Proof of staying in Belize (hotel reservation, a note from a host, etc.)

- A return or onward ticket.

- Proof of sufficient funds for the duration of the stay.

- A non-refundable visa processing fee.

Submission: Send the application and supporting paperwork to the nearest Belizean embassy or consulate. Processing times vary, so apply well in advance of your anticipated trip dates.

Upon arrival in Belize, visa holders must present their passport and visa to immigration agents, who will stamp the passport with the permissible term of stay, which is usually up to 30 days. If you want to extend your stay beyond the original period, you must apply for an extension at the nearest immigration office in Belize, which is usually granted in one-month increments for a modest fee.

2.2.2 Work and Residence Permits

If you wish to work, do business, or stay in Belize for a long time, you must get the necessary licenses. Here are the main types of permits and the processes involved:

Work Permits

Before working or conducting business in Belize, foreign people must get a work permit. There are several types of work permits, including self-employment, employment with a Belizean company, and temporary work permits for specific projects or activities.

Application Process:

Job Offer: Receive a job offer from a Belizean firm or develop a thorough business plan for self-employment.

Application Form: Obtain and fill out the work permit application form from the Department of Labour or their official website.

Supporting documents: Submit the following papers together with the completed application form:

- A valid passport with at least six months of validity remaining.

- Passport-sized photos.

- A police clearance certificate from your home country.

- A medical certificate demonstrating good health.

- Proof of job-related credentials and experience.

- A job offer letter or business plan.

- Payment of the application fee.

Submission & Processing:

- Submit the application and any supporting papers to the Department of Labor.

- The processing time for work permits might vary from a few weeks to many months. It is suggested that you apply well in advance of your desired start date.

Residency Permits

Belize offers many residency options for foreign nationals looking to live in the country on a long-term basis. These include the Qualified Retired Persons (QRP) Program, as well as Permanent and Temporary Residency.

Qualified Retired Persons (QRP) Program

- The QRP program, designed for retirees and those looking to spend their retirement years in Belize, offers a variety of benefits, including tax-free income generated outside of Belize and duty-free importation of personal items.

- Eligibility requirements include being at least 45 years old, receiving a monthly income of at least

USD 2,000 from a pension or annuity, and passing a background check.

Application Process:

Obtain and fill out the QRP application form from the Belize Tourism Board (BTB) or the official website.

Submit the completed form, along with the following documents:

- A valid passport
- Birth Certificate
- Marriage Certificate (if applicable)
- Proof of income (annuity or pension statements)
- Police clearance certificate
- Medical certificate
- Passport-sized photos
- Payment of the application fee

Permanent Residency:

Permanent residency allows foreign nationals to live and work in Belize permanently. To be eligible, you must have resided in Belize for at least a year without leaving the country for more than 14 consecutive days.

Application Process:

Obtain and fill out the Permanent Residence Application Form from the Department of Immigration.

Submit the completed form, along with the following documents:

- A valid passport
- Police clearance certificate
- Medical certificate
- Proof of financial stability (bank statements, job letters, etc.)
- Payment of the application fee

Temporary Residency:

Temporary residence is an option for those who want to stay in Belize for a prolonged period but do not meet the requirements for permanent residency. It is usually provided for one year and can be renewed annually.

Application Process:

Obtain and fill out the temporary residency application form from the Department of Immigration.

Submit the completed form, along with the following documents:

- A valid passport
- Police clearance certificate
- Medical certificate
- Proof of financial stability (bank statements, job letters, etc.)
- Payment of the application fee

2.3 Currency and Money Matters

When planning a vacation to Belize, it is important to understand the local currency, conversion rates, banking options, and budgetary issues. Proper financial planning can ensure a smooth and enjoyable holiday as you explore this vibrant Central American country.

2.3.1 Exchange Rates

The Belize dollar (BZD)

Belize's national currency is the Belize Dollar (abbreviated as BZD). The Belize Dollar's symbol is ordinarily "$," but to distinguish it from other dollar currencies, it is frequently written as "BZ$." The Belize Dollar is connected to the United States. Dollar (USD) at a fixed exchange rate of 2 BZD = 1 USD. This constant conversion rate simplifies financial transactions for tourists, particularly those from the United States because the currency is easy to understand and calculate.

Key Points About the Belize Dollar:

- **Denominations:** Belizean banknotes exist in denominations of $2, $5, $10, $20, $50, and $100, while coins come in 1 cent, 5 cents, 10 cents, 25 cents, 50 cents, and 1 dollar.

- **Currency Usage:** Although the BZD is the official currency, the U.S. Dollars are widely accepted across the country, especially in tourist destinations. Most prices at Belizean businesses are quoted in BZD, however, it is not uncommon for merchants to accept payments in USD and issue changes in BZD.

- **Cash vs. Card:** While credit and debit cards are becoming more widely accepted in urban areas and tourist destinations, cash remains the preferred method of payment in many sections of Belize, particularly in rural and remote villages.

Exchange Rate Stability and Market Rates

As stated, the exchange rate between the Belize Dollar and the U.S. The dollar is tied at 2 BZD to 1 USD. However, if you are converting other currencies, such as Euros (EUR), British Pounds (GBP), or Canadian Dollars (CAD), the pricing may differ depending on current market exchange rates and the institution providing the conversion service.

Where to Exchange Currencies:

- **Banks:** Major banks in Belize, including Belize Bank, Atlantic Bank, and Scotiabank, offer currency exchange services. It is easiest to convert money during standard banking hours (Monday through Friday, 8:00 AM to 4:00 PM).

- **Currency exchange offices** are typically found near airports, border crossings, and popular tourist destinations. While convenient, they may provide less attractive conversion rates than banks.

- **Hotels and Resorts:** Some hotels and resorts provide currency exchange services to their guests. However, hotels' exchange rates are typically less competitive than those offered by banks.

- **ATMs:** While not technically a currency exchange option, withdrawing local currency from an ATM using an international debit or credit card is another way to obtain BZD. The exchange rate provided by your bank is usually close to the official rate, although additional fees may apply (more on this in the Banking and ATMs section).

Tips on Currency Exchange

- **Avoid exchanging currency with street vendors:** While some may offer low pricing, it is best to use official exchange facilities to avoid counterfeit currency or unfair negotiations.

- **Keep small denominations:** Because many smaller businesses and vendors may not have change for large bills, it is suggested that you bring smaller denominations of BZD while shopping in markets or on public transportation.

- **Know the exchange rate:** Before converting money, examine current market rates online or using a financial app to see whether the rate you're provided is appropriate.

2.3.2 Banking & ATMs

Belize's financial system is substantially developed, particularly in metropolitan areas and popular tourist destinations. Understanding how to access your money and conduct financial activities while in Belize is critical for a stress-free stay.

Belize's Major Banks

Belize is home to various renowned banks that offer a wide range of services, including currency exchange, ATM withdrawals, and international banking. The most prominent banks in Belize are:

- **Belize Bank** is one of Belize's oldest and largest banks, with many locations and ATMs around the country. Belize Bank offers a variety of services, including currency exchange, international wire transfer, and Internet banking.

- **Atlantic Bank:** Another significant player in the Belizean banking sector, Atlantic Bank has a strong presence in major cities and provides services like currency exchange, ATM withdrawals, and Internet banking.

- **Scotiabank Belize:** As part of the global Scotiabank network, this bank offers a wide range of financial services, such as currency exchange, foreign transfers, and access to global banking facilities.

- **Heritage Bank,** a locally owned and operated bank, provides a range of services such as personal and commercial banking, currency exchange, and ATM access.

Accessing ATMs

ATMs (Automated Teller Machines) are widely available across Belize's major areas, including Belize City, Belmopan, San Pedro, Placencia, and Caye Caulker. However, they become less popular in rural and remote areas, therefore it is critical to plan your financial needs accordingly.

Key Points for Using ATMs in Belize:

Card Acceptance: Most ATMs in Belize accept foreign debit and credit cards, particularly those issued by Visa and MasterCard. Some ATMs may also accept American Express, albeit this is less common.

Withdrawal Limits: Daily withdrawal limits vary depending on the bank and card issuing organization. Typically, the limitation ranges from BZ$500 to BZ$1,500 each day.

Fees: When using an international card at a Belizean ATM, be mindful of the potential fees. This may include:

- The Belizean bank charges a fee for using their ATM. This fee typically ranges from BZ$3 to BZ$10 for each transaction.

- Your home bank charges you an international transaction fee when you use your card overseas. The cost varies depending on your bank's policies.

- Money Conversion Fee: Some banks charge a fee to convert your native currency into BZD.

Security: As with any abroad vacation, it is critical to use caution while using ATMs. Choose ATMs in well-lit, secure locations, such as bank branches, and avoid withdrawing large sums of money in public.

Traveler's Checks

Traveler's checks were formerly a popular way to transport money internationally, but their use has declined substantially due to the availability of ATMs and credit cards. While certain banks in Belize will still take traveler's checks, the process can be time-consuming, and they are not widely accepted by shops. If you bring traveler's checks, make sure they are in the United States. Dollars are most commonly accepted.

Credit and Debit Card Usage

Credit and debit cards are widely accepted in Belize, particularly at hotels, restaurants, and large retail establishments. However, there are a few important considerations to keep in mind:

- **Card Acceptance:** Visa and MasterCard are the most widely accepted credit cards in Belize. American Express and Discover are less commonly accepted, particularly in smaller places.

- **Foreign Transaction Fees:** Many credit card issuers charge a foreign transaction fee, which is typically between 1% and 3% of the purchase amount. Before going, verify with your card provider to understand any possible fees.

- **Notify Your Bank:** Before traveling to Belize, notify your bank or credit card issuer of your travel plans. This can assist keep your card from being flagged for suspicious activity when used internationally.

- **Security:** As with ATMs, use caution while using your credit or debit card. Keep your card in sight while making purchases, and check your account frequently for any unauthorized charges.

Mobile and Online Banking

Belize's leading banks provide mobile and online banking, allowing you to manage your cash while on the go. These services are especially useful for tracking your account balance, shifting payments, and paying bills. If you intend to

38

use online banking, ensure that you have access to a secure internet connection and consider using a VPN (Virtual Private Network) to protect your personal information.

2.4 Language and Communication

Effective communication is essential for a smooth and enjoyable travel experience, and understanding the linguistic environment of Belize will help you explore the country more easily. Belize's diverse cultural heritage is reflected in its languages, which include English as the official language as well as various other languages that are widely spoken.

2.3.3 Budgeting for Your Travel

Creating a suitable budget for your Belize holiday is critical to ensuring a pleasant and stress-free experience. Belize offers a wide range of experiences, from luxury resorts to affordable motels, so your budget will be determined by your travel style, tastes, and planned activities.

Accommodation Costs:

Accommodation in Belize varies substantially in price based on the kind of house and location. Here's an overview of hotel options:

Luxury Hotels and Resorts:

- **Price range:** $200 to $600 or more each night.

- **Amenities:** Luxury accommodations may include isolated beachside locations, high-end restaurants, spas, and personalized services. Ambergris Caye, Placencia, and private islands are popular destinations for luxury accommodations.

Mid-range Hotels and Boutique Resorts:

- **Price range:** $100-$200 per night.

- **Facilities:** Mid-range options frequently provide attractive hotels with amenities like pools, on-site eateries, and guided tours. These are popular in tourist destinations including San Ignacio, Hopkins, and Caye Caulker.

Budget Hotel and Hostel:

- **Price range:** $20-$80 per night.

- **Amenities:** Budget accommodations range from simple hotels and guesthouses to hostels with shared dormitory rooms. These accommodations are ideal for backpackers and budget-conscious travelers.

Vacation Rental and Airbnb:

- The price range varies greatly, ranging from $50 to $500+ every night.

- **Amenities:** Vacation rentals can range from modest flats to entire villas, providing flexibility for families and groups. Prices vary according to location, size, and amenities.

Food and Dining Costs

Belize features a vibrant culinary culture.

From street food to upscale dining. Here's a summary of what to anticipate in terms of eating expenses:

Street Food and Local Eateries:

- Prices range from $3 to $10 each dinner

- Options include local cuisine like fried jacks, tacos, rice and beans, and fresh seafood at reasonable pricing. Street sellers and tiny local restaurants (known as "comedones") are ideal for budget-conscious travelers.

Casual Dining and Mid-Range Restaurants:

- Price range: $10 to $30 each dinner.

- Options: Mid-range restaurants serve a variety of local and foreign cuisines for both lunch and dinner. These businesses frequently provide fresh fish, grilled meats, and local delicacies.

Fine-Dining and Gourmet Restaurants:

- Price range: $30 to $100+ each supper.

- Options: For a memorable night out, Belize's fine dining restaurants serve gourmet food, frequently with an emphasis on fresh, local ingredients. Expect to see them at popular tourist areas and high-end resorts.

Transportation Costs

Transportation rates in Belize might vary depending on how you choose to travel around.

Domestic flights:

- Price range: $50 to $150 for each flight.

- Domestic flights are the shortest way to travel between Belize City, San Pedro, Placencia, and Dangriga. Tropic Air and Maya Island Air provide regular flights.

Water Taxis:

- Prices range from $10 to $30 per trip.

- Water taxis are a popular mode of transportation for exploring the islands (cayes), including Ambergris Caye and Caye Caulker. The charge varies according to the distance and service provider.

Buses:

- Prices range from $2 to $10 every trip.

- Buses are the most cost-effective way to travel across the continent. Belize has a substantial bus system that connects major communities and cities, albeit the service may be slow and unpleasant.

Car Rental:

- Price range: $50-$100 per day.

- Renting a car allows you to explore at your own pace, particularly in areas such as the Cayo District and southern Belize. Be aware that road conditions may change, and 4WD vehicles may be required in certain areas.

Taxis:

- Prices range from $5 to $25 each ride.

- Taxis are widely available in urban regions and tourist destinations. Meters are rarely used, therefore always agree on a cost before commencing your journey.

Activity Costs

The cost of activities in Belize can vary significantly depending on the type of experience:

Guided Tours and Excursions

- Price range: $50 to $200 or more per person.

- Belize offers a wide range of guided activities, from seeing Mayan ruins and cave tubing to snorkeling and diving on the Barrier Reef. Prices vary depending on the activity, location, and if transportation and meals are included.

Independent Activities:

- Prices range from free to $50 per person.

- Several natural elements, such as beaches, hiking trails, and wildlife sanctuaries, may be explored independently. National parks and reserves have comparatively low entrance fees, ranging from $5 to $10 per person.

Water Sports and Equipment Rentals:

- Price range: $20 to $100 or more each day.

- Most coastal areas provide equipment rentals for sports such as kayaking, paddleboarding, and snorkeling. Prices vary depending on the kind of equipment and the duration of the rental.

Miscellaneous Costs

Travel Insurance:

- Price range: $50 to $150+ for standard insurance.

- Travel insurance is highly recommended to cover medical emergencies, trip cancellations, and lost luggage. The cost varies according to the coverage, the length of the trip, and the traveler's age and health.

Tipping:

- Tipping is encouraged but not required in Belize. In restaurants, a tip of 10% to 15% is typical. Tipping tour guides, taxi drivers, and hotel employees is entirely up to you and is determined by the level of service provided.

Souvenir & Shopping:

- Price range: $5 to $100 or more.

- Belize offers a variety of locally made items, including wood carvings, textiles, jewelry, and chocolate. Prices vary depending on the item and where you buy it (markets sometimes provide better deals than hotel gift shops).

Creating Your Budget

When deciding your trip budget, consider the following things.

- **Accommodation:** Choose the level of comfort and location that best suits your travel style. Tourists on a tight budget may prefer hostels or guesthouses, whilst those seeking luxury may opt for high-end resorts.

- **Dining:** Depending on your preferences, plan a variety of local eateries and dining experiences. Street food sampling is a great way to save money while also learning about local cuisine.

- **Transportation:** Consider how you want to get to Belize. If you want to visit several destinations, factor in the cost of flights, water taxis, and car rentals.

- **Activities:** Prioritize the experiences you want to have and spend your money accordingly. Some activities, such as diving in the Blue Hole or seeing remote Mayan ruins, may need a larger portion of your money.

- **Miscellaneous Expenses:** Remember to include travel insurance, gratuities, and souvenirs in your budget. It is also recommended to set aside some emergency funds.

2.4.1 Official Language

English: the official language

Belize's official language is English, making it the only Central American country with English as the primary language of government, education, and media. This is a big advantage for English-speaking tourists since it eliminates the language barrier that may exist in other parts of the region.

Key Points About English in Belize:

- **Government and Administration:** All official documents, government forms, judicial proceedings, and public signage are written in English. This makes it easier for tourists to do administrative activities like completing out immigration papers, learning local laws, and following directions.

- **Belize's education system** uses English as the language of teaching from basic to postsecondary levels. As a result, most Belizeans speak English fluently, making communication easier for English-speaking visitors.

- **Media and Entertainment:** The majority of media sources in Belize, including newspapers, television, and radio, use English as their primary language. Tourists would be able to easily access news and entertainment in English.

Creole: The Lingua Franca

Although English is the official language, the majority of the population speaks Belizean Creole (Kriol). Creole is frequently utilized in informal discussions and is the primary language spoken by many Belizeans in their everyday life. It is an English-based language with elements of African, Spanish, and other languages, reflecting the country's varied background.

Key Points of Belizean Creole:

- **Features:** Belizean Creole is an English-based Creole language, therefore English speakers may frequently comprehend it, albeit pronunciation, syntax, and vocabulary may differ greatly from Standard English. For example, the English word "they" becomes "deh" in Creole, and "What are you doing?" becomes "What do you do?"

- **Cultural Significance:** Creole is more than just a language; it is an essential part of Belizean identity

49

and culture. Understanding and using even a few Creole words may allow travelers to connect more deeply with the local culture and people.

- **Use in Daily Life:** Creole is commonly used in marketplaces, on public transportation, at home, and among friends. While most Belizeans can easily switch between Creole and Standard English, they often use Creole in informal settings.

Spanish and Other Languages

Belize is a diverse country whose population includes Mestizo, Maya, Garifuna, and other ethnic groups. As a result, several other languages are spoken in addition to English and Creole.

Spanish:

- **Prevalence:** Spanish is Belize's second most widely spoken language, mostly in the northern and western regions bordering Mexico and Guatemala. Many Belizeans are bilingual, speaking English and Spanish fluently.

- **Usage:** Spanish is often spoken in homes, businesses, and schools in areas with a large Mestizo population. Even though English is the official language, you may encounter Spanish in informal settings, particularly in markets, rural areas, and among older generations.

Maya Languages:

- **Languages:** Belize has three main Mayan languages: Yucatec, Mopan, and Kekchi. The Maya people speak these languages in the country's south and west.

- **Cultural Importance:** The use of Mayan languages is typically associated with the preservation of historic rituals, rites, and communal life. While tourists are unlikely to need to learn Mayan languages, understanding their importance in Belizean culture might enhance your vacation experience.

Garifuna:

- **Language and Culture:** The Garifuna people, who live mostly in southern Belize (e.g., Dangriga and Hopkins), speak the Garifuna language, which has roots in Arawakan, Carib, and European languages.

- **Use in Daily Life:** Garifuna is used in the home and cultural expressions like music, dance, and ritual. Like the Mayan languages, it has more cultural importance than a language that tourists must learn.

Communication in Tourism Areas

English is widely spoken in tourist destinations like Ambergris Caye, Placencia, and Caye Caulker. Hotel employees, tour guides, and shopkeepers are accustomed to dealing with English-speaking customers, which makes communication simpler. However, in more remote areas, particularly those with large indigenous populations, you may encounter locals who speak little English. In such cases, a few lines in Creole or Spanish might be highly useful.

2.4.2 Common Phrases and Expressions

Learning a few local terms will enhance your vacation experience in Belize, allowing you to converse more politely with the locals and manage daily situations more easily. Here are some easy phrases in both Belizean Creole and Spanish that may come in handy:

Belize Creole Phrases

- Hello / "Hail up" or "Weh di go aan?"

- How are you?: " How yuh di go?"

52

- I am OK, thank you: "Ah good, tanks."

- What is your name?" Weh yuh name?"

- My name is: "Mi name da…"

- Please: "Please" (just like in English)

- Thank you: "Tanks".

- You are welcome: " No wahn" or "Yuh welcome"

- Goodbye: "Latta" or "Mi Gaan"

- Yes: "Yes" or "Eh-eh".

- No: "No" or "Nuh-uh".

- Where are…?"Weh, deh?""

- How much does it cost?: "How much dis cost?"

Spanish Phrases

- Hello / "Hola"

- How are you?: "Cómo estás?"

- "Estoy bien, gracias."

- What is your name?" Cómo te llamas?"

- My name is "Me llamo…"

- Please say "Por favor"

- Thank you: "Gracias".

- You are welcome: "De nada"

- Goodbye: "adiós"

- Yes: "Sí"

- No: "No"

- Where are...?"Dónde está...?""

- How much does it cost?" Cuánto cuesta esto?"

Tips for Effective Communication

- **Speak Slowly and Clearly:** Although English is widely spoken, many Belizeans speak it as a second language. Speaking slowly and clearly may help avoid misunderstandings.

- **Use Simple Language:** Avoid employing complex language or idioms that cannot be translated properly. Simple, clear language is often the most effective.

- **Be Patient and Polite:** Demonstrating patience and courtesy, especially when there is a language barrier, goes a long way toward creating positive experiences.

- **Learn Key Words:** Making an effort to learn a few Creole or Spanish terms can make you more appealing to locals and express your appreciation for their culture.

2.5 Health and Safety Tips

Health and safety are critical when traveling and understanding the necessary procedures and local standards will help ensure a safe and healthy stay in Belize.

2.5.1 Vaccination and Health Precautions

Recommended Vaccines

Before traveling to Belize, ensure that your routine vaccinations are up to date and consider additional vaccines based on the risks associated with travel to Central America. The Centers for Disease Control and Prevention (CDC) and the World Health Organization (WHO) recommend the following vaccines for tourists to Belize.

- **Routine vaccines:** Make sure you are current on routine immunizations such as:

- **Measles, Mumps, and Rubella (MMR):** Vaccination is essential due to measles' resurgence over the world.

- **Diphtheria, Tetanus, and Pertussis (DTaP):** Tetanus is especially important if you plan to participate in outdoor activities.

- Varicella (chickenpox)

- Polio

- **Influenza:** Especially important if traveling during the flu season.

Hepatitis A&B:

- **Hepatitis A** vaccination is recommended for all travelers since the virus can be transmitted through contaminated food and drink.

- **Hepatitis B:** Especially recommended for anybody who may be exposed to blood or bodily fluids (e.g., healthcare workers, and people seeking medical treatment).

Typhoid:

Typhoid fever can be contracted by contaminated food or water. This immunization is especially recommended if you plan to dine at a small establishment where sanitary controls may be less stringent.

Rabies:

Rabies is widespread in Belize, particularly among animals and stray dogs. While the risk to most visitors is low, vaccination is recommended for anyone planning to participate in outdoor activities like caving, camping, or hiking where they may be exposed to animals.

Malaria Prophylaxis:

Malaria is an issue in certain parts of Belize, particularly in rural regions. Although the overall risk is low, you should consider taking antimalarial medication if you plan to go to areas where malaria is common. Consult your healthcare provider to choose the best medicine and dosage.

Water and Food Safety

Water Safety:

- In Belize, tap water is frequently unsafe to drink unless boiled or filtered beforehand. It is preferable to use bottled or filtered water, which is readily available. Avoid ice in beverages unless you know it's made from pure water.

Food Safety:

- Be cautious when eating street food or meals from local vendors. Ensure that the meal is freshly prepared and served hot. Stick to peelable fruits and avoid raw or undercooked meats.

Insect-borne Diseases

Dengue Fever:

- Dengue is a mosquito-borne illness that is common in Belize. Dengue has no vaccine, thus prevention is based on avoiding mosquito bites. When visiting dengue-endemic areas, use insect repellent, wear long-sleeved clothing, and sleep under a mosquito net.

Zika Virus:

- Mosquitoes also carry Zika, which can cause birth defects if pregnant women become infected. If you are pregnant or want to become pregnant, you should avoid traveling to areas where Zika is a danger. Follow the same precautionary actions as for dengue.

Sun Exposure and Dehydration

Sun Protection:

- Belize has a tropical environment with plenty of sun exposure. To protect yourself from UV rays, use high-SPF sunscreen, a wide-brimmed hat, and sunglasses. Regularly reapply sunscreen, especially after swimming or sweating.

Hydration:

- Staying hydrated is essential, especially if you are participating in outdoor activities. Carry a water bottle and drink enough fluids throughout the day to avoid dehydration.

2.5.2 Safety Guidelines and Local Laws

General Safety Tips

- Belize is generally a safe destination for tourists, but like in any country, there are areas where caution is required. Following these safety considerations may help ensure a safe and enjoyable stay.

Stay Informed:

- Keep up to date on travel advisories in the areas you want to visit and contact local authorities or hotel personnel if you encounter any safety concerns.

Avoid flashy displays of wealth

- Petty theft and pickpocketing may occur, particularly in congested areas. Avoid displaying expensive jewelry, cameras, or large quantities of money. For valuables, keep them in a money belt or concealed bag.

Be cautious at night

- While many tourist attractions are safe, it's best to avoid walking alone at night, especially in unfamiliar or poorly lit areas. To go about after dark, choose a licensed cab or a reputable public transportation option.

Secure your belongings

- Keep your hotel room closed, and use the in-room safe to store passports, money, and other valuables. Do not leave your belongings unattended at the beach or pool.

Respect local customs

- Belize is a diverse country with a diversity of cultures and customs. Being aware of local traditions, such as dressing modestly in certain places, might help you avoid unwanted attention or misunderstandings.

Local Laws and Customs

Understanding and adhering to local legislation is critical to staying safe and avoiding legal issues throughout your trip:

Drug Laws:

- The possession and use of illegal substances are strictly prohibited in Belize. Drug offenses can result in serious penalties, including longer prison sentences. Marijuana is decriminalized in small amounts for personal use, but public usage remains illegal.

Alcohol consumption:

- Belize's legal drinking age is 18. Public drinking is discouraged, and it is illegal to consume alcohol in public places unless permitted (for example, at licensed events or venues). Drink responsibly and be aware of your surroundings.

Environmental Protection:

- Belize places a strong priority on environmental conservation. It is illegal to collect coral, shells, or other natural items from beaches or marine areas. Littering is also banned, and violators may face punishment.

Photography:

- While photography is often encouraged, please obtain permission before photographing individuals, especially in rural areas or among indigenous groups. Some cultural sites may restrict photography, so be sure to follow any posted signs or guidelines.

Driving Laws:

- If you decide to rent a car, keep in mind that you must drive on the right side of the road. Seat belts are required, and using a mobile phone while driving is not permitted. Speed limits are enforced, particularly in metropolitan areas and around schools.

2.5.3 Travel Insurance

Importance of Travel Insurance

- Travel insurance is an important part of trip planning since it may protect you against unforeseen events such as medical emergencies, trip cancellations, lost luggage, and other travel-related issues. Given the variety of activities and potential risks in Belize, comprehensive travel insurance is strongly recommended.

What Your Travel Insurance Should Cover

When selecting a travel insurance policy, ensure that it covers the following crucial areas.

Medical Coverage:

- Make sure your insurance covers medical care, hospital stays, and emergency medical evacuation. This is especially important in Belize, where medical facilities may be few in rural areas and evacuation to another country (e.g., Mexico or the United States) may be necessary in extreme circumstances.

Adventure Activities:

- If you wish to do adventurous sports like scuba diving, snorkeling, zip-lining, or hiking, be sure your insurance policy covers them. Certain plans may require a higher premium for high-risk sports.

Trip Cancellation or Interruption:

- Trip cancellation coverage reimburses you if you have to cancel your trip due to a covered cause such as illness, accident, or unforeseeable situations like natural catastrophes. Travel interruption coverage compensates you if your travel is cut short due to an emergency.

Lost or Delayed Baggage:

- This coverage provides payment for lost, stolen, or delayed baggage, allowing you to replace important items until your bags are returned to you.

Personal Liability:

- If you accidentally cause property damage or harm to another person, personal liability insurance can protect you from legal claims and expenses.

How to Choose a Policy.

When acquiring travel insurance coverage, consider the following suggestions:

Compare Providers:

- Compare plans from several insurance providers to find one that provides the most coverage at a reasonable cost. Look for customer reviews and consider the provider's reputation for claim handling.

Understand Exclusions:

- Be aware of any policy restrictions, like pre-existing medical conditions, high-risk activities that are not covered, or coverage limits for certain locations. Ensure that the insurance meets your specific needs.

Emergency Assistance Services:

- Choose insurance that provides 24-hour emergency assistance. This might be vital in the event of an emergency, providing aid with medical evacuations, lost passports, or other critical situations.

Policy Documentation:

- Keep a copy of your travel insurance policy, as well as emergency contact information, in a secure area during your trip. It's equally critical to communicate this information with a reliable friend or family member back home.

Making a claim

If you need to submit a claim for your travel insurance, follow these steps:

- **Contact Your Insurance Provider:** Notify your insurance provider as soon as possible after an incident. They will guide you through the claims process and notify you of any essential documents.

- **Maintain all documentation:** Gather and keep all relevant documents, such as medical records, receipts, police reports, and proof of purchase for lost or stolen items. These will be required to support your claim.

- **Submit Your Claim Quickly:** Submit your claim as quickly as possible, following the provider's instructions. Delays in filing a claim may result in issues or even rejection of the claim.

- **Follow-up:** Stay in touch with your insurance provider to ensure that your claim is being handled. Be patient yet persistent if necessary, and keep records of all communications.

Planning a holiday to Belize requires precise planning to ensure a smooth and enjoyable experience. Everything is vital, from choosing the best time to go and understanding admission procedures to managing your funds, health, and safety. Being well-informed and prepared allows you to fully immerse yourself in Belize's vibrant culture, breathtaking environment, and many activities.

3. Getting to Belize

Belize, a small but dynamic Central American country, has several convenient entry points and transit options for both foreign and domestic travelers. Whether you arrive by air, land, or sea, understanding the numerous options and processes will allow you to plan your trip with ease. This section provides a detailed guide on landing in Belize and visiting the country while you're there.

3.1 Airports & Airlines

3.1.1 Major International Airports

Belize has one major international gateway, the Philip S.W. Goldson International Airport (BZE), located at Ladyville, just outside of Belize City. This airport is the primary entry point for most international visitors, connecting Belize to major cities in North America, Central America, and the Caribbean.

Philip S. W. Goldson International Airport (BZE):

- **Location:** The Philip S.W. Goldson International Airport, located around 10 miles (16 kilometers) from Belize City, is Belize's busiest airport, handling practically all international flights.

- **Facilities and Services:** Currency exchange, ATMs, duty-free retailers, restaurants, and car rental firms are among the services offered at the airport. Despite its small size in comparison to major international hubs, the airport provides essential services to passengers.

- **Airlines and Destinations:** Several major airlines fly to and from BZE, connecting Belize to important locations in North America and the Caribbean. American Airlines, Delta, United, and Southwest offer direct flights from Miami, Dallas, Houston, and Atlanta. Additionally, smaller carriers such as Tropic Air and Maya Island Air provide connections to neighboring Central American countries as well as internal destinations inside Belize.

- **Customs & Immigration:** Upon arrival, travelers will be required to provide their passport and, if appropriate, a visa. The procedure is pretty straightforward, and English-speaking professionals are available to assist.

Placencia Airport(PLJ):

- **Location:** The Placencia Airport, located in southern Belize, serves the well-known Placencia

Peninsula and is an important gateway for travelers to the area.

- **Facilities:** The airport is small and only serves domestic flights, although it is an important link for people heading to or from the country's southern area. There are limited amenities, however the airport is conveniently located close to resorts and tourist attractions.

- **Flights:** Tropic Air and Maya Island Air fly frequently between Placencia and the Philip S.W. Goldson International Airport, as well as other domestic destinations. This airport provides easy access to the beaches and marine parks of southern Belize.

San Pedro airport (SPR):

- **Location:** San Pedro Airport is located on Ambergris Caye, one of Belize's most popular tourist destinations. The airport serves as a vital link between the island and the mainland.

- **Facilities:** San Pedro Airport is small but well-maintained, with minimal amenities including a waiting area, restrooms, and a few businesses. It is located within walking distance of several hotels and resorts in San Pedro Town.

- **Flights:** Tropic Air and Maya Island Air offer regular flights to and from Belize City, making it easy for visitors to reach this island haven. The flight from Belize City to San Pedro is short, usually lasting about 15 minutes.

3.1.2 Domestic Flights

Domestic air travel in Belize is a convenient and popular way to see the country's many regions. Tropic Air and Maya Island Air, Belize's two largest domestic airlines, offer dependable flights connecting the country's mainland, islands, and remote areas.

Tropical Air:

- **Overview:** Tropic Air, founded in 1979, is Belize's largest and most established airline, offering both domestic and regional flights. Tropic Air has a fleet of small aircraft, providing regular flights to both major tourist destinations and more remote locales.

- Tropic Air serves popular destinations such as Belize City, San Pedro (Ambergris Caye), Caye Caulker, Placencia, Dangriga, and Punta Gorda. It also offers regional flights to Honduras, Guatemala, and Mexico.

- **Booking and Services:** Tickets may be purchased online, through travel agencies, or directly at the airport. Tropic Air provides a flexible schedule with many daily flights, making it easy for clients to plan their trips.

Maya Island Air:

- Overview: Maya Island Air is another major local airline in Belize, known for its great service and extensive network. It operates similarly to Tropic Air, offering flights within Belize and to select international destinations.

- Maya Island Air serves several locations, including Belize City, San Pedro, Caye Caulker, Placencia, and Punta Gorda. It also operates flights to the nearby Mexican city of Mérida.

- Like Tropic Air, tickets for Maya Island Air can be purchased online, at the airport, or through travel agents. The airline's frequent flights and reliable service make it a popular choice for both tourists and locals.

Tips For Domestic Air Travel:

- **Luggage restrictions:** Due to the small size of the aircraft, luggage restrictions are more stringent than on international flights. Typically, each passenger can bring one checked bag weighing up to 40 pounds (18 kg) and one carry-on. Excess baggage may incur additional fees and be shifted to a later plane.

- **Flight Duration:** Domestic flights in Belize are quick, lasting between 15 minutes to an hour, depending on the destination. The spectacular flights over Belize's coastline, cayes, and jungle are a bonus, providing breathtaking aerial views.

- **Check-In:** Passengers are urged to be at the airport at least 45 minutes to an hour before their aircraft departs. Check-in is usually quick and easy, but it's critical to be on time, especially if you're connecting to a foreign aircraft.

3.2 Land Border Crossings

For people arriving by land, Belize has borders with Mexico to the north and Guatemala to the west and south. Many land border crossings are often used by travelers, each with its own set of procedures and concerns.

3.2.1 Entry and Border Procedures

Northern Border: Belize—Mexico (Santa Elena Border):

- **Location:** The principal land crossing between Belize and Mexico is located at Santa Elena, between the cities of Corozal (Belize) and Chetumal (Mexico). This crossing is the most popular for those traveling from or to the Yucatán Peninsula, including Cancún, Playa del Carmen, and Tulum.

- **Border Facilities:** The Santa Elena border is well-equipped with customs and immigration offices on both sides. There are money exchange offices, food vendors, and transportation services such as buses and taxis.

- **Procedures:** Travelers entering Belize from Mexico must have a valid passport and, if necessary, a visa. Mexican nationals and residents of certain countries are permitted to enter Belize without a visa for short stays. When entering Belize, you must complete a customs declaration form and may be subjected to a baggage inspection. Products that exceed the duty-free quota must be disclosed.

- **Transportation:** Buses and shuttles regularly run between Chetumal and Belize City, including stops in Corozal and Orange Walk. Taxis are also available for shorter trips, such as to Corozal or nearby hotels.

Western Border: Belize–Guatemala (Benque Viejo del Carmen Border):

- **Location:** The main border crossing between Belize and Guatemala is at Benque Viejo del Carmen, near Melchor de Mencos, Guatemala. This bridge is the primary route for people traveling to and from the Guatemalan city of Flores and the renowned Maya ruins of Tikal.

- **Border services:** Both sides of the Benque Viejo del Carmen border have immigration and customs services. While the facilities are more modest than those along Mexico's northern border, they are functional and, on average, efficient.

- **Procedures:** Like the northern border, passengers entering Belize from Guatemala must provide a passport and, if necessary, a visa. Guatemalan natives and residents of certain countries are permitted to enter Belize without a visa for short stays. Customs procedures are straightforward, with luggage checks and the necessity to declare any purchases that exceed the duty-free limit.

- **Transportation:** Regular buses and shuttles connect Flores, Guatemala, and Belize City, including stops in San Ignacio and Belmopan. Taxis and private shuttles are also available, particularly for trips to nearby destinations such as San Ignacio and the Guatemalan border town of Melchor de Mencos.

Belize's southern border with Guatemala (Punta Gorda):

- **Location:** The southernmost land crossing between Belize and Guatemala is near Punta Gorda in the Toledo District. This crossing is less popular with travelers, but it is a viable option for those traveling between southern Belize and Guatemala's Izabal Department, which includes the town of Puerto Barrios.

- **Border amenities:** The Punta Gorda border crossing is simple and basic, with limited facilities. However, it serves its purpose for immigration and customs processing.

- **Procedures:** Entry is the same as at other land crossings, with travelers required to provide a passport and, if necessary, a visa. Given the low volume of traffic at this border, customs clearance is frequently expedited.

- **Transportation options** are restricted at this crossing. Boats also go between Punta Gorda and Puerto Barrios, providing a scenic and alternative route for holidaymakers.

General Tips for Land Border Crossings

- **Border Hours:** Land crossings are typically open from early morning until late evening, however, it is critical to confirm the exact hours of operation before traveling, especially on public holidays.

- **Crossing Fees:** Some border crossings charge a small departure or entry fee. It's a good idea to bring some local currency or US dollars to cover any expenses that may arise.

Safety: While Belize's borders are usually safe, it's important to keep alert and aware of your surroundings. Avoid crossing borders late at night and consider using a reliable transportation company.

3.3 Transportation in Belize

Once in Belize, there are a variety of transportation options available for getting through the country. Depending on your location and interests, you may navigate Belize's diverse topography via public transportation, car rentals, or even water taxis and ferries.

3.3.1 Public Transportation

Public transportation in Belize is a low-cost and extensively used option, particularly for those coming on a budget or wanting to experience the local way of life. Buses and taxis are the two most common modes of public transit, each with its own set of advantages and limitations.

Buses:

- Buses are the most common means of public transportation in Belize, providing frequent service between major towns and cities as well as more rural areas. The bus network covers much of the country, making it a viable option for many people.

- **Types of Buses:** Belize's bus system includes both standard buses (usually converted school buses) and more deluxe express buses. Regular buses are the most popular, with frequent stops and longer rides, but express buses provide faster, more direct routes with fewer stops.

- Major bus routes include the Northern Highway (Belize City to Corozal), the Western Highway (Belize City to San Ignacio and Benque Viejo), and the Hummingbird Highway (Belize City to Dangriga and Punta Gorda). These routes connect most of Belize's major cities and tourist destinations.

- **Fares and Tickets:** Bus fares are reasonable, with pricing varying according to the distance traveled. Tickets are often purchased directly from the driver or conductor on the bus. Except for some express routes where tickets can be reserved in advance, there is no need to book ahead of time.

- **Timetables and Frequency:** Buses run frequently, particularly along important routes, with services starting early in the morning and running until early evening. However, timetables are subject to change, and buses may only leave when they are full, so some patience is required.

- **Comfort and Safety:** While buses in Belize are generally safe, they might be overcrowded and lack air conditioning. You must keep your belongings safe and remain aware of your surroundings, especially on prolonged trips.

Taxis:

- **Availability:** Taxis are widely available throughout Belize's towns and cities. They may be flagged down on the street, found at taxi stands, or rented through hotels and resorts.

- **Costs:** Taxi prices in Belize are not metered, therefore you must agree on a fee with the driver before commencing your trip. Fares are generally reasonable, however, they might vary depending on the route, time of day, and driver.

- **Safety:** Taxis in Belize are generally safe, however, it is advisable to use licensed taxis, particularly in Belize City. Look for taxis with green license plates, which indicate that they have been licensed by the government. If you're unsure about a taxi's legitimacy, request a reference from your hotel.

- **Shared Taxis:** In some areas, particularly in rural areas, shared taxis (also known as "collectivos") are common. These taxis, like buses, transport a group of passengers along a predetermined route. They offer a more cost-effective option, especially for short excursions.

3.3.2 Car Rentals and Driving Tips

Individuals seeking greater independence and flexibility may find that renting a vehicle in Belize is the best option. It allows you to explore the nation at your leisure and visit more remote locations that may not be easily accessible by public transportation.

Car Rental:

- **Availability:** Car rental services are available in major towns and cities such as Belize City, San Ignacio, and Placencia. Rental companies include both well-known brands like Hertz and Budget, as well as local businesses.

- **Requirements:** To lease a car in Belize, you must have a valid driver's license from your home country. Most rental companies require drivers to be at least 25 years old, while some may rent to younger drivers at an additional cost.

- **Vehicles:** A variety of vehicles are available for hiring, ranging from little cars to 4x4 SUVs. Given the condition of certain roads in Belize, particularly in rural areas, renting a 4x4 vehicle is recommended if you want to visit off-the-beaten-path destinations.

- **Insurance:** Rental companies in Belize often give basic insurance with the option to purchase additional coverage. It's critical to thoroughly read the terms and conditions and consider purchasing comprehensive insurance for peace of mind.

- **Cost:** Car rental costs in Belize vary depending on the kind of vehicle, the length of the rental, and the season. To get the greatest rate, make your reservations ahead of time, especially during peak tourist seasons.

Driving Tips:

- **Road Conditions:** Belize's principal roads, including the Northern, Western, and Hummingbird highways, are normally in great condition. However, minor roads, particularly in rural areas, may be rough, unpaved, and poorly marked. Be prepared for potholes, unpaved areas, and little bridges.

- **Driving Laws:** In Belize, you drive on the right side of the road. Speed limits are enforced, particularly in metropolitan areas and around schools. The standard speed limit on roadways is 55 mph (88 km/h), however, in cities and villages, it is reduced to 25 mph (40 km/h).

- **Safety:** Always wear your seatbelt and avoid using your phone while driving. It is critical to remain vigilant, especially at night when road lighting is weak and animals or people may be on the roadway.

- **Fuel:** Gas stations are available in most cities and along major routes, while they may be scarce in more remote areas. It's critical to fill up your tank whenever possible, especially if you're traveling to rural or less-populated areas.

- **Navigation:** GPS devices and online maps are necessary for navigating Belize's roads, but it's also a good idea to have a physical map, especially if you're visiting areas with poor phone coverage. Road signs may be few, so pay close attention to landmarks and, if necessary, ask people for directions.

3.3.3 Water Taxi and Ferry

Given Belize's extensive coastline and numerous islands, boat transportation is essential for moving about, especially if you're visiting popular destinations such as Ambergris Caye, Caye Caulker, or the southern coastal districts.

Water Taxis:

- Water taxis are a popular and convenient way to travel between the mainland and the islands. They offer daily cruises between Belize City and the main cayes, which include Ambergris Caye and Caye Caulker.

- The two main water taxi companies are the San Pedro Belize Express and the Ocean Ferry Belize. Both businesses provide frequent daily departures on spacious boats that can accommodate large groups of people.

- **Routes and Destinations:** Popular routes include Belize City to San Pedro (Ambergris Caye), Belize City to Caye Caulker, and Caye Caulker to San Pedro. Some water taxis also connect with smaller islands and make stops along the way.

- **Tickets and Booking:** Tickets may be purchased at the water taxi stations, online, or through travel agencies. During peak tourist season, it is essential to make reservations ahead of time. The trip from Belize City to San Pedro typically takes around 1.5 hours, with a shorter 45-minute cruise to Caye Caulker.

- **Cost:** Water taxis are inexpensive, making them an affordable option for island-hopping. Round-trip tickets are often given at a discount.

- **Baggage:** Most water taxis can accommodate luggage, but it's best to travel light because the boats can become overcrowded during peak hours. Larger equipment, such as bicycles or surfboards, may incur additional costs.

Ferries:

- **Overview:** Ferries provide another option for getting between the mainland and the islands, particularly for those traveling to the southern coastal regions. They are less regular than water taxis, but they might be a useful option for specific routes.

- **Routes:** The main ferry route connects Punta Gorda in southern Belize to Puerto Barrios in Guatemala. This service is popular with travelers who travel between southern Belize and Guatemala's Caribbean coast.

- **Booking:** Ferry tickets may be purchased at the port or through travel agencies. It is critical to confirm the schedule in advance, as ferry services may be less frequent and subject to weather conditions.

General Tips for Water Travel

- **Weather:** Belize's weather may be variable, particularly during the rainy season. Water taxis and ferries may have delays or cancellations due to severe waves or storms, so check the weather forecast and plan accordingly.

- Life jackets are often provided on water taxis and ferries, but it is always a good idea to confirm that safety equipment is available and in good condition.

If you are prone to seasickness, consider taking medication before your vacation.

- **Timing:** Arrive at the terminal at least 30 minutes before your scheduled departure time, especially during peak hours. Boarding is often on a first-come, first-served basis, and boats can fill up quickly.

In conclusion, whether you arrive in Belize by air, land, or sea, understanding the various transportation options will help you see the country efficiently and enjoyably. Domestic flights provide beautiful aerial views, while buses provide a true local experience. Each mode of transportation has its perks. By correctly preparing your holiday, you may ensure a pleasant and stress-free trip, allowing you to fully immerse yourself in Belize's beauty and culture.

4. Accommodations

Belize offers a diverse range of hotel options to suit all budgets and interests, from lavish resorts nestled in lush rainforests or perched on private islands to basic guesthouses and budget-friendly hostels that allow you to experience the country's unique character without breaking the bank. Whether you're looking for elegance, comfort, or a simple place to stay, Belize has options for everyone.

4.1 Hotel and Resort

Belize is known for its beautiful and diverse scenery, which is complemented by a variety of hotels and resorts that provide excellent service and amenities. From high-end luxury resorts to comfortable mid-range hotels, you'll find accommodations to fit your needs and expectations.

4.1.1 Luxury Options

Luxury hotels and resorts provide an unequaled combination of comfort, elegance, and breathtaking settings for tourists looking to experience the best that Belize has to offer. These high-end residences usually have private villas, infinity pools, gourmet restaurants, and personalized services to meet your every need.

Ambergris Caye

- **Victoria House Resort & Spa:** This exquisite resort on Ambergris Caye is one of Belize's most luxurious hotels. Victoria House offers a variety of accommodation options, including stunning casitas and private villas, set against a backdrop of gorgeous sandy beaches and azure waters. Guests may savor exquisite food at the Palmilla Restaurant, unwind by the infinity pool, or indulge in spa treatments. The resort also provides close access to the Belize Barrier Reef, making it an excellent choice for diving enthusiasts.

- **Matachica Resort & Spa:** A boutique resort known for its vibrant decor and tranquil surroundings, Matachica Resort & Spa offers an exceptional holiday experience. The resort's thatched-roof villas have bright, contemporary decor that provides a stylish contrast to the surrounding natural splendor. Matachica also features a well-known spa, an award-winning restaurant, and a private beach with direct access to the Caribbean Sea.

Placencia

- **Naia Resort & Spa:** Located on the Placencia Peninsula, Naia Resort and Spa offers an unforgettable experience in a peaceful beachfront setting. The resort has large beach houses with private pools, a world-class spa, and a variety of sports such as kayaking, paddleboarding, and yoga. Naia's restaurant serves fresh, regionally inspired cuisine, and the resort's commitment to sustainability adds to its appeal.

- **The Turtle Inn,** owned by director Francis Ford Coppola, is an eco-luxury resort that combines rural beauty with modern amenities. The coastal resort offers Balinese-style villas with their own balconies and outdoor showers. Guests may enjoy gourmet cuisine at The Mare Restaurant, which specializes in seafood and organic vegetables, or unwind at the outdoor spa. Turtle Inn also serves as a gateway to the neighboring coral reefs and the Cockscomb Basin Wildlife Sanctuary.

Cayo District

- **Blancaneaux Lodge:** Another Coppola property, Blancaneaux Lodge is located in the remote Mountain Pine Ridge Forest Reserve. The resort's exquisite cabanas and villas overlook Privassion Creek, providing a peaceful retreat surrounded by nature. Guests may explore nearby waterfalls, enjoy horseback riding, or relax in the resort's hot pool. The lodge's restaurant serves Italian-inspired cuisine prepared with vegetables from the resort's organic garden.

- **Chaa Creek Lodge** is a pioneer in eco-tourism, offering luxury accommodations with a focus on sustainability. The lodge's thatched-roof suites and villas are set in a remote nature reserve along the Macal River, offering the ideal combination of luxury and adventure. Guests may participate in guided tours of the reserve, see the on-site Maya temple, or unwind in the spa. Chaa Creek's restaurant serves organic, farm-to-table cuisine, and the resort is committed to environmental stewardship and community involvement.

4.1.2 Mid-Range Options

For travelers looking for comfort without breaking the bank, Belize has a variety of mid-range hotels and resorts that provide excellent value for money. These accommodations typically combine modern amenities with local charm, making them ideal for families, couples, and solo travelers alike.

San Ignacio:

- **San Ignacio Resort Hotel:** Overlooking the Macal River, the San Ignacio Resort Hotel is a family-owned establishment that offers comfortable accommodations with an air of elegance. The hotel has a variety of rooms and suites, a swimming pool, a tennis court, and a restaurant serving Belizean and foreign cuisine. The property's green grounds are home to an on-site iguana conservation program, providing visitors with a unique experience.

- **Cahal Pech Village Resort:** Named after the nearby Maya ruins, Cahal Pech Village Resort offers a peaceful retreat with panoramic views of the Belize River Valley. The resort's thatched-roof cabanas and modern suites are surrounded by tropical gardens, creating a relaxing atmosphere. Guests may relax in the outdoor pools, dine in the open-air café, or take a short walk to the Cahal Pech ancient site.

Hopkins:

- **Jaguar Reef Lodge & Spa:** Located in the coastal village of Hopkins, Jaguar Reef Lodge & Spa offers beachfront accommodations with a welcoming atmosphere. The resort offers rooms, suites, and private villas, many with ocean views and direct beach access. Guests may enjoy sports like snorkeling, fishing, and kayaking, or simply relax by the pool or at the spa. The on-site restaurant serves fresh seafood and Belizean favorites.

- **Hamanasi Adventure & Dive Resort:** Hamanasi is a boutique resort that caters to adventure seekers, offering a variety of outdoor activities such as scuba diving, snorkeling, trekking, and birdwatching. The resort's features include treehouse rooms and beachfront suites, all designed with comfort and sustainability in mind. Hamanasi's restaurant serves farm-to-table meals, and the resort's commitment to environmentally friendly practices has earned it several awards.

Belize City:

- **The Radisson Fort George Hotel & Marina** is a popular mid-range option in Belize City, offering modern amenities and convenient access to the city's attractions. The hotel features beautiful rooms and suites, two swimming pools, a fitness center, and a variety of dining options. It's a popular choice for both business travelers and tourists, with convenient access to the Belize Barrier Reef and other local attractions.

- **Best Western Plus Belize Biltmore Plaza:** This hotel provides comfortable accommodations and excellent service at an affordable price. The Belize Biltmore Plaza features a swimming pool, fitness center, and restaurant, making it an ideal choice for travelers looking to stay in Belize City. The hotel also offers a variety of excursions and activities, such as visits to local Maya ruins and river cruises.

4.2 Budget Accommodation

Belize offers a variety of budget-friendly hotel options, such as hostels, guesthouses, and inns. These low-cost options provide a lovely place to stay while allowing you to enjoy the country's distinct culture and natural beauty without spending a fortune.

4.2.1 Hostels

Hostels are a popular choice for backpackers, solo travelers, and those looking to meet other like-minded tourists. Belize's hostels are typically located in desirable neighborhoods close to attractions and offer a wide range of amenities such as dormitory-style dorms, individual rooms, community kitchens, and common areas.

Ambergris Caye.

- **Sandbar Beachfront Hostel & Restaurant:** Located near the beach in San Pedro, Sandbar is a thriving hostel that offers both dormitory and private rooms. The hostel features a seaside bar and restaurant, a communal kitchen, and a rooftop patio with stunning views of the Caribbean Sea. It's an excellent choice for budget travelers looking to enjoy the island's nightlife and water sports.

- **Pedro's Inn Backpackers Hostel** is a low-cost hostel in San Pedro that offers simple, clean accommodations. The hostel offers dormitories, individual rooms, and a swimming pool. It is known for its laid-back atmosphere, and guests may take advantage of the on-site bar and pizza. Pedro's Inn is conveniently located near the beach and other San Pedro attractions.

Caye Caulker:

- **Pause Hostel:** A local family owns an eco-friendly hostel in Caye Caulker, which supports an animal rescue program. Pause Hostel offers dormitory beds and private rooms in a tranquil beachfront setting. The hostel has a communal kitchen, hammocks for lounging, and kayaks available to guests. It's an excellent choice for budget vacationers looking to enjoy Caye Caulker's laid-back atmosphere.

- **Bella's Backpackers** is a popular hostel on Caye Caulker that offers a variety of accommodations, including dormitory beds, private rooms, and cabins. The hostel features a common kitchen, a rooftop patio, and hammocks for resting. Bella's is known for its welcoming atmosphere, making it an ideal location for meeting other travelers and exploring the island together.

San Ignacio:

- **Hi-Et Guesthouse:** Hi-Et Guesthouse is a low-cost option in the heart of San Ignacio. The guesthouse offers modest rooms with shared or private bathrooms. It's conveniently located near restaurants, shopping, and the San Ignacio Market. The courteous staff can help you plan tours to nearby attractions like the Actun Tunichil Muknal cave or the Xunantunich Maya site.

- **Tropicool Hotel** is a small, inexpensive hotel located in downtown San Ignacio. The hotel offers clean and basic rooms with fans or air conditioning. The principal attractions of the town, such as the Cahal Pech ruins and the San Ignacio market, are within walking distance. Tropicool is an ideal choice for travelers looking for affordable accommodation with easy access to the area's attractions.

4.2.2 Guest Houses and Inns

Guesthouses and inns provide a more intimate and often more personalized experience than larger hotels. They are frequently family-owned and offer a warm, welcoming atmosphere. These hotels are ideal for guests looking to experience Belize's local culture and hospitality on a budget.

Placencia:

- **Sailfish Resort** is a low-cost inn located in the heart of Placencia Village. The resort offers a variety of housing options, including private rooms, suites, and self-catering apartments. Guests may relax by the pool, drink at the bar, or visit the nearby beaches and restaurants. Sailfish Resort is known for its friendly service and relaxed atmosphere, giving it an ideal location for touring Placencia.

- **Seaspray Hotel:** Seaspray Hotel is a beachfront hotel in Placencia that offers inexpensive accommodations with spectacular views of the Caribbean Sea. The hotel offers a range of lodgings, from basic to more luxurious, all only feet from the beach. Guests may enjoy the on-site restaurant, hire bicycles to explore the area, or simply relax on the beach. Seaspray is a popular choice for budget-conscious travelers looking for beachfront accommodations.

Hopkins:

- **Palmento Grove Lodge** is a cultural and environmentally sustainable guesthouse located in Hopkins' Garifuna settlement. The resort offers rustic accommodations in traditional thatched-roof cabanas, offering guests a true flavor of Garifuna culture. Guests may participate in cultural events including drumming sessions and traditional cuisine classes, as well as explore the nearby beaches and woods. Palmento Grove is ideal for people who want to immerse themselves in Belizean culture on a budget.

- **All Seasons Guest House** is a charming, family-run guesthouse located in Hopkins. The guesthouse offers simple yet pleasant rooms with private bathrooms and air conditioning. The beach and local cafés are also within walking distance. The friendly proprietors can help plan tours and activities, making it an excellent base for exploring the surrounding area.

Cayo District:

- **Parrot Nest Lodge** is a one-of-a-kind, low-cost guesthouse located near San Ignacio in the Cayo District. The resort includes treehouse-style cottages set in a magnificent tropical garden, providing a peaceful retreat surrounded by nature. Guests may relax in hammocks, explore the adjacent river, or join guided tours to nearby attractions. Parrot Nest Lodge is ideal for nature lovers and budget travelers looking for a unique holiday in Belize.

- **Lower Dover Field Station & Jungle Lodge:** Lower Dover is an eco-friendly hostel located on the Belize River in the Cayo District. The resort offers rustic accommodation in a natural setting, with easy access to hiking trails, swimming areas, and Maya ruins. Guests may enjoy home-cooked meals, learn about the local flora and fauna, and explore the neighboring forest. Lower Dover is a great option for budget travelers looking for an off-the-beaten-path adventure.

4.3 Unique Stays

For travelers seeking a more unconventional experience, Belize has a variety of unique housing options that go beyond the typical hotel or resort. Whether you want to stay in an eco-lodge surrounded by nature, a boutique hotel with personalized charm, or a vacation rental that feels like a home away from home, Belize offers a variety of options for a wonderful stay.

4.3.1 Eco-Lodges

Eco-lodges in Belize are ideal for ecologically aware visitors who want to be in harmony with nature while exploring the country's many ecosystems. These lodges are frequently located in remote areas such as rainforests, nature reserves, or near historic Maya ruins, allowing guests to connect with Belize's natural splendor in an immersive and sustainable way.

Cayo District:

- **Chaa Creek Lodge:** Located on the banks of the Macal River, Chaa Creek Lodge is one of Belize's most well-known ecotourism destinations. This award-winning property is located inside a private 400-acre natural reserve and offers beautiful, eco-friendly accommodations ranging from thatched-roof cottages to treetop suites. The resort supports sustainability and conservation by providing activities including guided nature treks, birdwatching, and river paddling. Chaa Creek's organic farm provides fresh food for the restaurant and the resort participates in a variety of community and environmental initiatives.

- **The Lodge at Big Falls** is located in southern Belize, near Punta Gorda, and offers eco-friendly accommodation on a calm riverside. The resort features private cabanas with thatched roofs and modern amenities, all designed to blend in with the surrounding jungle. Guests may visit neighboring Maya sites, go bird-watching, or enjoy water activities like kayaking and tubing on the Rio Grande River. The Lodge at Big Falls is committed to sustainable tourism practices and actively supports local communities via various programs.

Toledo District:

- **Cotton Tree Lodge:** Located on the banks of the Moho River in Toledo District, Cotton Tree Lodge is a remote eco-lodge that offers an immersive experience in the Belizean jungle. The lodge's rustic thatched cabanas are surrounded by lush rainforests, and the property's commitment to sustainability is evident in its use of solar energy, rainwater collecting, and organic farming. Guests may participate in activities including chocolate-making courses, guided forest excursions, and cultural tours to nearby Maya settlements. Cotton Tree Lodge is ideal for people looking to unplug from the modern world and reconnect with nature.

Mountain Pine Ridge:

- **Blancaneaux Lodge:** Owned by filmmaker Francis Ford Coppola, Blancaneaux Lodge is located in the Mountain Pine Ridge Forest Reserve and offers a wonderful eco-friendly retreat. The lodge's cabanas and villas are made of indigenous materials and are tucked among the stunning natural backdrop of waterfalls, rivers, and pine trees. Blancaneaux Lodge emphasizes sustainability through hydroelectric energy, organic gardening, and a commitment to preserving the local nature. Guests may explore the surrounding Rio Frio Cave, see the Caracol Maya ruins, or simply relax in the lodge's hot pool.

4.3.2 Boutique Hotels

Boutique hotels in Belize provide a unique and personalized experience, often defined by exquisite design, small settings, and attentive service. These hotels are often smaller than regular resorts, allowing for a more intimate and personalized experience. Many boutique hotels in Belize are located in picturesque settings such as beaches, islands, or old cities.

Ambergris Caye.

- **El Secreto** is a boutique resort located on Ambergris Caye's northern tip, offering an exclusive and beautiful refuge. The resort consists of separate villas with modern décor, each with its own plunge pool and outdoor shower. The villa is surrounded by magnificent gardens and offers breathtaking views of the Caribbean Sea. El Secreto's personalized service, calm atmosphere, and attention to detail make it a top choice for couples and honeymooners looking for a romantic getaway.

- **The Phoenix Resort,** located in the center of San Pedro, is a boutique hotel that combines contemporary luxury with a tranquil island atmosphere. The resort's spacious suites include stylish decor, fully outfitted kitchens, and private balconies with ocean views. Guests may relax in the hotel's infinity pool, visit the on-site spa, and dine on gourmet cuisine. The Phoenix is known for its excellent service and convenient location, making it an ideal base for touring Ambergris Caye.

Placencia:

- **Turtle Inn:** Turtle Inn, another of Francis Ford Coppola's boutique resorts, is located in Placencia and offers a blend of rustic charm and refined grandeur. The resort's Balinese-style bungalows and villas are set among tropical gardens and provide direct access to the beach. Turtle Inn's customized service, world-class cuisine, and tranquil setting make it an excellent choice for tourists looking for a boutique experience in southern Belize. The resort's commitment to sustainability and emphasis on local culture add to its appeal.

- **Laru Beya Resort** is a boutique oceanfront resort located on the Placencia Peninsula. The resort offers a variety of accommodations, ranging from one-bedroom apartments to three-bedroom penthouses, all with balconies or terraces. The property features a swimming pool, a restaurant serving Belizean and international cuisine, and a variety of activities such as snorkeling, diving, and cultural excursions. Laru Beya's relaxed atmosphere and personal service make it a popular choice for families and couples alike.

Caye Caulker:

- **Weezie's Ocean Front Hotel and Garden Cottages** offers a boutique experience on the relaxed island of Caye Caulker. The resort offers a variety of accommodations, including oceanfront suites, garden cottages, and a private beachfront house. The hotel's décor is bright and cheerful, evoking the island's vibrant personality. Guests may relax by the pool, ride about the island, or participate in water activities like snorkeling and paddleboarding. Weezie's personalized service and intimate setting make it a popular choice for travelers looking for a one-of-a-kind stay on Caye Caulker.

4.3.3 Vacation Rentals

Vacation rentals in Belize provide the independence and comfort of a home away from home. Whether you're traveling with family, or a group of friends, or seeking a longer stay, vacation rentals provide the space and facilities you need to enjoy your time in Belize at your leisure. Belize's Liberty vacation rentals range from beachfront homes to jungle cabins, catering to a wide variety of interests and budgets.

Ambergris Caye.

- **Villa Incommunicada:** This wonderful beachfront property on Ambergris Caye offers the perfect environment for a tranquil and relaxing vacation. The residence has five bedrooms, a fully equipped kitchen, an infinity pool, and breathtaking views of the Caribbean Sea. Guests may appreciate the ease of having their own space while being only a short drive from San Pedro's eateries and sights. Villa Incommunicado is suitable for families or parties looking for a secluded, self-contained getaway.

- **Casa de Bonita** is a wonderful vacation home located on Ambergris Caye's north end. The villa features three bedrooms, a private pool, and direct beach access, making it an excellent choice for anyone looking to explore the island's natural beauty in a tranquil environment. The property is built with modern facilities, and its open layout is excellent for families or small gatherings.

Placencia:

- **Swan Villas,** located on the Placencia Peninsula, provides a collection of one-of-a-kind holiday houses designed in a distinctive, organic architectural style. Each villa features large living areas, modern kitchens, and private patios with views of the lagoon or the Caribbean Sea. The villas have great amenities such as private pools and jacuzzis, and guests can take advantage of the property's closeness to the beach and Placencia Village. Swan Villas is suitable for those searching for a mix of luxury and individual taste.

- **Ranguana** is a beachfront vacation home in Placencia, only steps away from the Caribbean Sea's azure waves. The house features three bedrooms, a fully equipped kitchen, and an outside living area with a private pool. Guests may enjoy easy beach access while being near Placencia Village's restaurants and services. Villa Ranguana is great for families or groups seeking a calm and expansive beach vacation.

San Ignacio:

- **Cayo Vista Guesthouse** is a tourist establishment on the outskirts of San Ignacio that offers a tranquil refuge with stunning views of the surrounding mountains and valleys. The guesthouse offers a variety of bedrooms, a fully supplied kitchen, and outdoor sitting areas, making it suitable for families and groups. Guests may enjoy the peaceful settings while being only a short drive from San Ignacio's attractions, such as the Xunantunich Maya site and the Green Iguana Conservation Project.

- **Mountain Equestrian Trails:** For tourists seeking a one-of-a-kind experience in the Cayo District, Mountain Equestrian Trails offers vacation housing on a working ranch. The property features rustic cottages surrounded by woodlands and pastureland, making it ideal for a natural vacation. Guests may go horseback riding, bird watching, and take guided excursions of surrounding caves and waterfalls. Mountain Equestrian Trails is great for anyone seeking an exciting, off-the-grid adventure.

Belize's hotels serve a wide range of guests, from luxury resorts and eco-friendly lodges to low-cost hostels and unusual vacation rentals. Whether you want comfort, adventure, or a combination of the two, Belize has a wealth of alternatives to improve your vacation experience. Wherever you choose to stay, you will be met with warmth and charm that reflect the vibrant nature of this magnificent country.

5. Exploring Belize

5.1 Popular Destinations

Belize boasts a rich cultural past, stunning terrain, and a diversified animal species. Each area is distinct, making it a popular destination for travelers with diverse interests. Whether you're drawn to the historical beauty of Belize City, the frenetic nightlife of San Pedro, or the tranquil beaches of Ambergris Caye, Belize has something for everyone. This section will look at two of the most popular places, Belize City and San Pedro, and provide a detailed review of their attractions and activities.

5.1.1 Belize City

Belize City, the country's biggest metropolis and former capital, serves as a cultural and historical center. Although many people utilize it as a gateway to other regions of the country, the city itself has a rich history, with various attractions that explore Belize's colonial past and colorful culture.

5.1.1.1 Historical Sites

Belize City is home to some of the country's most significant historical landmarks, which shed light on colonial history and the march to freedom.

St. John's Cathedral:

St. John's Church, Central America's oldest Anglican church, was constructed between 1812 and 1820 using bricks supplied as ballast on ships from England. This historic edifice is significant not just for its architecture, but also because it was the scene of consecutive Mosquito Coast kings' coronations by British officials. The cathedral's interior, which has mahogany seats and stunning stained-glass windows, provides insight into Belize's religious and colonial past. The nearby Yarborough Cemetery, Belize's oldest cemetery, has a long history and houses the remains of many of the city's early immigrants.

Government House (House of Culture):

Government House, today known as the House of Culture, was formerly the residence of the British Governor of British Honduras. This colonial mansion, constructed in 1814, is one of Belize City's most important structures and depicts the British colonial period. Today, the House of Culture is a museum and cultural center with exhibits on Belize's colonial history, route to independence, and cultural heritage. The magnificently landscaped gardens and historical structures make this a must-see trip for history buffs.

Swing Bridge:

The Swing Bridge in downtown Belize City is one of only a few manually operated swing bridges worldwide. The bridge, erected in 1923, spans Haulover Creek and links the city's northern and southern halves. It swings open twice a day to allow boats to pass through, a tradition that has continued to this day. The bridge honors the city's maritime history while also acting as a functional piece of Belizean heritage.

Baron Bliss Lighthouse:

The Baron Bliss Lighthouse, located near the entrance of Belize Harbor, functions as both a memorial and a working lighthouse. It was created to honor Baron Henry Edward Ernest Victor Bliss, a British-born philanthropist who left a considerable portion of his fortune to Belizeans. Baron Bliss never visited Belize, but he fell in love with the country while moored offshore. The lighthouse and the nearby Baron Bliss tomb are popular tourist sites that provide panoramic views of the Caribbean Sea.

5.1.1.2 Museums and Cultural Centers

Belize City's museums and cultural institutions provide a thorough overview of the country's rich history, from its Maya roots to its colonial past and dynamic multicultural present.

Museums in Belize:

The Museum of Belize, housed in a former colonial jail, is one of the city's most famous cultural institutions. The museum presents a complete picture of Belizean history, with displays covering the ancient Maya culture, the colonial period, and the country's march to freedom. The edifice itself is a piece of history, with strong brick walls and iron-barred windows that serve as memories of its past purpose. Inside, visitors may look at a variety of exhibits, including Maya artifacts, historical records, and a collection of colonial-era stamps and coins. The museum often hosts temporary exhibitions that highlight current Belizean art and culture.

Belize City House of Culture and Downtown Rejuvenation Project:

This continuing initiative seeks to rebuild Belize City's downtown while retaining its historical and cultural significance. The House of Culture, housed in the ancient Government House, is the focal point of this endeavor. It functions as a cultural center, presenting exhibitions, conferences, and performances that promote Belize's distinct cultural milieu. The project also involves the restoration of historic structures and the establishment of public areas to honor the city's rich heritage. Visitors can explore the House of Culture's exhibitions, attend cultural events, or simply meander around the refurbished downtown area, which blends history and modern life.

Bliss Institute of Performing Arts:

The Bliss Institute for Performing Arts, named for Baron Bliss, is Belize City's main cultural venue. The organization provides a diverse range of cultural events, including theatrical productions, concerts, dance performances, and art exhibitions. It also contains the Belize National Art Collection, which includes works by renowned Belizean painters. The Bliss Institute fosters and maintains Belizean culture, making it an essential visit for anybody interested in the country's creative and cultural life.

Image Factory Art Foundation:

The Image Factory Art Foundation, a modern art gallery and cultural institution in Belize City, has been at the forefront of the country's art scene since its establishment in 1995. The gallery hosts exhibitions by recognized and new Belizean artists in a variety of genres, including painting, sculpture, digital art, and photography. The Image Factory also functions as a cultural center, offering lectures, seminars, and events addressing Belize's social and cultural issues. The Image Factory is a must-see for art lovers and anybody interested in modern Belizean culture.

5.1.2 San Pedro (Ambergris Caye)

San Pedro, located on the southern side of Ambergris Caye, is one of Belize's most popular tourist sites. San Pedro, with its magnificent beaches, active nightlife, and closeness to the Belize Barrier Reef, provides a traditional Caribbean experience. The town's relaxed environment, along with its diverse activities and sights, makes it a popular destination for travelers.

5.1.2.1 Beach and Water Activities

Ambergris Caye is linked with sun, sea, and sand, while San Pedro provides access to some of Belize's most spectacular beaches and marine activities.

Hol Chan Marine Reserve:

The Hol Chan Marine Reserve is a popular snorkeling and diving location in the San Pedro region. This protected area, located just a short boat trip from town, is part of the Belize Barrier Reef Reserve System, a UNESCO World Heritage site. Hol Chan, which translates to "Little Channel" in Maya, is a natural incision in the reef that supports a diverse diversity of marine life. Snorkelers and divers may explore spectacular coral formations, swim amid tropical fish schools, and even encounter larger species like nurse sharks and stingrays. The reserve is separated into zones that provide different underwater experiences, from coral gardens to mangrove forests.

Shark Ray Alley:

Shark Ray Alley, located next to the Hol Chan Marine Reserve, is another excellent snorkeling spot. This shallow site is well-known for its resident nurse sharks and southern stingrays, who are accustomed to seeing humans. Snorkelers may feel elated after swimming with these friendly creatures in crystal-clear water. Shark Ray Alley is typically featured on Hol Chan excursions, making it a must-see for anybody seeking close contact with Belize's aquatic fauna.

Secret Beach:

Despite its name, Secret Beach is no longer a secret, yet it remains one of the greatest spots to spend a quiet day on the beach. Secret Beach, located on Ambergris Caye's western side and away from the bustling town center of San Pedro, offers peaceful, shallow waters suitable for swimming and sunbathing. The beach has become a popular destination for both locals and tourists, with a selection of beachside taverns and restaurants where you can have a refreshing drink or a meal while your toes are in the sand. Kayaking and paddleboarding are other popular activities here, making it an excellent choice for both leisure and adventure.

Mexico Rocks:

Mexico Rocks is another great snorkeling area north of San Pedro. This area contains a cluster of coral heads in relatively shallow water, making it suitable for snorkelers of all skill levels. The coral formations here are stunning, and the area is teeming with marine life, including colorful fish, spiny crabs, and a rare turtle. Mexico Rocks was named a marine reserve in 2015, assuring the preservation of this flourishing underwater environment.

Dive The Belize Barrier Reef:

Ambergris Caye has some of the best scuba diving possibilities in the Western Hemisphere. The Belize Barrier Reef, the world's second-largest barrier reef, is just a short boat trip from San Pedro. Dive sites including the Blue Hole, Turneffe Atoll, and Lighthouse Reef are well-known for their spectacular underwater beauty and varied marine life. Whether you're a novice or an experienced diver, San Pedro has some of the most breathtaking and unique diving experiences.

5.1.2.2 Nightlife and Entertainment

San Pedro is more than just daytime activities; at night, the town comes alive with a thriving nightlife scene that has something for everyone. San Pedro has a lot to offer, whether you want to dance all night, listen to live music, or simply relax with a beer by the sea.

Fido's Courtyard and Pier:

Fido's Courtyard is one of San Pedro's most popular bars and live music venues. Fido's, located on the beach in the heart of town, has a lively environment with regular live music performances ranging from reggae and calypso to rock and blues. The bar offers a broad range of beverages, including tropical cocktails and Belizean beers, and the outside setting is great for a night out. Fido's is a popular hangout for both locals and visitors, making it an ideal location for meeting new people and experiencing the island's nightlife.

The Palapa Bar & Grill:

For a more relaxing evening, head to the Palapa Bar & Grill, which is popular with both locals and visitors. This tavern, perched above the coast, provides breathtaking views of the Caribbean Sea as well as a peaceful, welcoming ambiance. The Palapa Bar is famed for its "floating tubes," in which you may lie in an inner tube and have a drink brought to you from a bucket dropped from the bar. The menu combines Belizean and foreign cuisine, and the bar regularly hosts live music and events. The Palapa Bar is the perfect location to unwind after a day touring the island.

Secret Beach Sunset Bar:

If you're visiting Secret Beach in the late afternoon, the Secret Beach Sunset Bar is the place to go. As the name suggests, this oceanfront bar is a wonderful spot to view the sunset over Ambergris Caye's peaceful waters. The pub provides a range of beverages, beers, and snacks, and its casual environment makes it a favorite hangout for both locals and visitors. Whether you're enjoying a drink from a beach chair or taking a plunge in the gentle surf, the Secret Beach Sunset Bar is the perfect way to conclude your day on Ambergris Caye.

Soca Nights at Jaguar's Temple:

If you want to dance the night away, Jaguar's Temple is the place to be. This well-known nightclub is famous for its "Soca Nights," where you may dance to the enticing rhythms of soca, reggae, and dancehall music. The club has a huge dance floor, a rooftop lounge, and several themed events throughout the week. Jaguar's Temple is a popular spot for people wishing to experience San Pedro's lively nightlife.

The Truck Stop:

The Truck Stop is a unique entertainment business that has swiftly gained popularity on Ambergris Caye. This food truck park provides a wide variety of dining options, including wood-fired pizzas and Asian fusion cuisine, as well as a complete bar serving unique drinks and local breweries. In addition to wonderful cuisine and drinks, The Truck Stop provides a variety of activities, including outdoor movie nights, trivia contests, and live music performances. The

Truck Stop's tranquil, family-friendly ambiance makes it an excellent spot to spend an evening with friends or family.

Casino Action:

For those feeling lucky, San Pedro features a few small casinos where you may try your luck at poker, blackjack, and slots. While not the same size as casinos in major cities, these venues offer a nice and calm gaming environment. The environment is inviting, and the stakes are minimal, making it suitable for both serious gamblers and those seeking entertainment.

Island Bar Crawl:

One of the most popular ways to enjoy San Pedro's nightlife is to participate in an island bar crawl. These guided excursions take you to some of the island's top bars and clubs, providing an overview of the local nightlife culture. Along the way, you'll meet other travelers, drink different beverages, and dance to live music. Bar crawls are a great opportunity to see the island's nightlife in a relaxed and inviting setting, and they typically include visits to some of San Pedro's greatest places.

5.1.3 Caye Caulker

Caye Caulker, a small island off the coast of Belize, is ideal for people wanting a laid-back atmosphere, abundant marine life, and a strong sense of community. The island's slogan, "Go Slow," appropriately depicts the relaxed pace of life here. Caye Caulker, albeit smaller and less developed than its neighbor Ambergris Caye, provides a more intimate and authentic experience, making it a popular destination for hikers, divers, and anybody wishing to decompress.

5.1.3.1 Snorkeling and Diving Spots

Caye Caulker's proximity to the Belize Barrier Reef makes it a perfect location for snorkeling and diving aficionados. The island is bordered by the Caribbean's most pristine and accessible marine environments.

The split:

The Split is a natural waterway that divides Caye Caulker in half and is one of the island's most popular attractions. This location is perfect for swimming, snorkeling, or just resting by the water. The clear, shallow waters support a varied assortment of marine life, including colorful fish and coral formations. The Split also has a well-known beach bar where you may have a refreshing drink while admiring the sun and the quiet island atmosphere.

Coral Garden:

Coral Gardens, just a short boat trip from Caye Caulker, is a popular snorkeling spot noted for its colorful coral formations and rich aquatic life. The region is teeming with colorful fish, sea fans, and sponges, making it an ideal underwater destination for snorkelers. Coral Gardens is ideal for snorkelers of all ability levels because of its modest depths and calm waters. Guided tours are available, which give information on the reef's ecosystem and the species that reside there.

Caye Caulker Marine Reserve:

The Caye Caulker Marine Reserve, established in 1998, preserves a part of the Belize Barrier Reef and its surrounding environment. The reserve features seagrass meadows, mangroves, and coral reefs, all of which provide critical habitat for a wide variety of marine organisms. Snorkeling and diving in the reserve allow you to observe everything from little seahorses and schools of tropical fish to larger species like rays and sharks. The reserve is separated into zones, each of which offers a distinct experience, such as coral gardens, seagrass meadows, and mangrove forests.

Hol Chan Marine Reserve and Shark Ray Alley:

Despite their proximity to Ambergris Caye, the Hol Chan Marine Reserve and Shark Ray Alley are popular day-trip options from Caye Caulker. Hol Chan is recognized for its rich biodiversity, with the possibility to see a variety of fish, rays, and even the uncommon manatee. Shark Ray Alley, as previously said, provides a unique snorkeling experience among nurse sharks and stingrays. Guided trips from Caye Caulker often include both destinations, delivering an unparalleled marine experience.

5.1.3.2 Relaxation and wellness

Caye Caulker is more than just an adventure destination; it's also a place to relax and refresh while taking advantage of the island's "Go Slow" philosophy.

Yoga and Wellness Retreats:

Caye Caulker has become a favorite location for yoga and wellness enthusiasts. Several yoga studios and health resorts provide training and courses in serene outdoor settings, sometimes with views of the ocean. Whether you're a seasoned yogi or a beginner, the island's quiet atmosphere is great for reconnecting with your body and mind. Many retreats provide holistic therapies, such as massages and meditation sessions, to help guests relax and unwind.

Beachside Spas:

Caye Caulker's oceanfront spas provide a variety of treatments, including deep-tissue massages, facials, and body scrubs. The calming sound of the waves and mild sea wind add to the relaxing experience, leaving you feeling refreshed and energized. These spas usually employ natural, locally sourced products, like coconut oil and seaweed, to produce treatments that highlight the island's inherent beauty.

The Lazy Lizard:

The Lazy Lizard, located in The Split, is more than simply a bar; it is the island's hub for leisure and social activities. With its magnificent setting, the Lazy Lizard is the ideal spot to relax with a drink in hand, watch the sunset, and meet other tourists. The bar's laid-back, welcoming environment makes it a favorite hangout, and the famous "Lizard Juice" cocktail is a must-try. The Lazy Lizard represents Caye Caulker's laid-back character, whether you're lounging on the beach or floating in the lovely waters of The Split.

Island Walks and Sunsets:

A leisurely walk around Caye Caulker is one of the simplest yet pleasurable pleasures. The island is small enough to explore on foot, and walking along its sandy roads allows you to fully appreciate its natural beauty. As the day comes to a close, head to the western side of the island to see some of Belize's most breathtaking sunsets. The combination of the setting sun, the peaceful ocean, and the island's tranquil ambiance makes for a wonderful experience.

5.1.4 Placencia

Placencia is a charming peninsula in southern Belize noted for its stunning beaches, vibrant culture, and broad range of activities. The peninsula is approximately 16 kilometers long, with the Caribbean Sea on one side and a quiet lagoon on the other. Placencia Village, located on the peninsula's southern tip, is the principal tourist destination, combining old majesty with modern luxury. Placencia has something for everyone, whether they wish to be adventurous or relaxed.

5.1.4.1 Outdoor Activities

Placencia serves as the gateway to some of Belize's most magnificent adventures, both on land and at sea.

Snorkeling and diving in the Belize Barrier Reef:

The Belize Barrier Reef is easily accessible from Placencia, making it an excellent choice for snorkeling and diving aficionados. Whale shark sightings are common around the

Gladden Spit and Silk Cayes Marine Reserve during the season (March to June). These gentle giants, the world's largest fish, visit the region to feed on spawning fish, offering divers an exceptional experience. In addition to whale sharks, the reefs surrounding Placencia sustain a wide variety of marine life, including magnificent corals, tropical fish, and larger species including rays and turtles.

Monkey River Wildlife Tours:

Monkey River, a short boat ride from Placencia, is a favorite spot for animal experiences. The river flows through a dense jungle, providing a home for a diverse range of wildlife, including howler monkeys, crocodiles, iguanas, and several bird species. Guided journeys down the river allow you to witness these animals in their natural surroundings. The travels often include a visit to the little village of Monkey River, where you may learn about the local culture and way of life.

Kayak and Paddleboard:

The calm waters of Placencia's lagoon are suitable for kayaking and paddleboarding. Exploring the lagoon by kayak or paddleboard takes you up close to the mangroves, where you may observe manatees, birds, and other animals. Many local tour companies provide guided tours that teach about the lagoon's biodiversity and the role of mangroves in preserving the shoreline. For those seeking a bit more adventure, sea kayaking cruises are offered that take you along the peninsula's shores and out to nearby cayes.

Hiking at Cockscomb Basin Wildlife Sanctuary:

The Cockscomb Basin Animal Sanctuary, just a short drive from Placencia, is one of Belize's top hiking and animal viewing sites. The sanctuary, which features the world's first jaguar refuge, spans around 150 square kilometers of tropical rainforest. Hiking trails of various difficulty weave through the forest, allowing visitors to see a diverse range of wildlife, including jaguars (though sightings are uncommon), ocelots, peccaries, and a variety of bird species. The refuge also has several waterfalls and natural ponds where you may cool yourself after your hike.

Sailing and Island hopping:

Placencia is a good starting place for sailing trips across Belize's southern cays. Sailing cruises transport you to peaceful islands and coral atolls where you may swim, fish, and relax on gorgeous beaches. Many cruises include stops on uninhabited islands where you may admire the beauty of the Belize Barrier Reef in seclusion. Whether you're on a day trip or a multi-day sailing holiday, the crystal-clear waters and diverse marine life make for an amazing experience.

5.1.4.2 Arts and Crafts

Placencia is more than simply an adventure destination; it is also a center for arts and crafts, with a flourishing community of local artisans and a rich cultural heritage.

Placencia Sidewalk:

The Placencia Sidewalk, which runs through the heart of Hamlet, is officially designated as the world's tiniest road. This charming pedestrian promenade is studded with boutiques, cafés, and art galleries, making it an ideal spot for discovering the local arts and crafts scene. Handcrafted things available here include jewelry, paintings, wood carvings, and fabrics, many of which are inspired by Belize's natural beauty and cultural diversity. The sidewalk is also home to a variety of street vendors selling anything from fresh coconut water to locally produced cuisine.

Lola's Art Gallery:

Lola's Art Gallery is one of Placencia's most well-known art galleries, displaying the works of local artist Lola Delgado. Lola's bright paintings showcase the spirit of Belize, including local people, animals, and the environment. Handcrafted jewelry and pottery are among the items on display at the gallery. Visiting Lola's Art Gallery allows you to support local artists while also bringing home a unique piece of Belizean art.

Garifuna Cultural Center:

Placencia's Garifuna Cultural Center promotes a greater understanding of the Garifuna people, who are derived from African, Carib, and Arawak ancestors. The center presents presentations about Garifuna's story, culture, and customs, including music, dancing, and food. Visitors may learn about the Garifuna's traditional art forms, including drumming, storytelling, and crafts. The center also hosts discussions and performances that provide an entertaining approach to learning about Garifuna culture.

Maya House of Cacao:

The Maya House of Cacao, located just outside of Placencia, offers a unique viewpoint on both traditional and contemporary chocolate-making techniques. The center exhibits the history of cacao in the Maya civilization, from its use as currency to its importance in ceremonies and festivals. Visitors may see demonstrations of traditional chocolate-making processes and sample a range of chocolate treats created with locally sourced cocoa. The Maya House of Cacao also features a gift shop where visitors may purchase handcrafted chocolates and other cacao-based items.

5.1.5 Hopkins

Hopkins is a tiny beach village in southern Belize recognized for its diverse cultural legacy, particularly the Garifuna people. The village is recognized as the "Cultural Capital of Belize" and provides tourists with a complete experience of Garifuna culture, including music, dance, and cuisine. Hopkins, in addition to its cultural attractions, is a gateway to some of Belize's most breathtaking natural environments, making it a must-see destination for visitors looking to immerse themselves in both culture and the environment.

5.1.5.1 Garifuna Culture and Heritage

Hopkins is one of the best sites in Belize to experience the colorful culture of the Garifuna, who have maintained their customs and way of life for decades.

Garifuna Drums and Dance:

Garifuna drumming and dance are integral to the community's cultural expression. The beats of Garifuna drums, particularly the "Segunda" and "primero" drums, are fundamental to many parts of Garifuna culture, including religious ceremonies and social events. Visitors to Hopkins can witness live drumming performances, which are frequently accompanied by traditional dances such as the "Punta" and "Jankunu." Several cultural centers and lodges in the village offer drumming workshops, where you can learn the fundamentals of Garifuna drumming and even participate in a group performance.

Lebaha Drum Centre:

The Lebaha Drumming Middle, located in the center of Hopkins, is a cultural institution committed to the preservation and promotion of Garifuna drumming and music. The center provides drumming lessons, cultural tours, and live performances, giving visitors a thorough grasp of Garifuna music and its significance in the community. The Lebaha Drumming Center also engages in educational initiatives, working with local schools to guarantee that the next generation continues the Garifuna musical culture.

Garifuna Settlement Day:

Garifuna Settlement Day, celebrated annually on November 19th, is one of Hopkins' and Belize's most well-known cultural events. The ceremony honors the Garifuna people's entrance into Belize in the early nineteenth century and includes a variety of traditional activities such as reenactments of the landing, parades, drumming, dancing, and feasting. Hopkins is an excellent site to mark Garifuna Settlement Day since the entire community comes together to honor their heritage. Visitors are welcome to join in the celebrations, which offer a delightful cultural experience.

5.1.5.2 Local Culinary Experiences

Garifuna cuisine is an essential element of the Hopkins cultural experience, with traditional dishes highlighting the community's African, Caribbean, and indigenous origins.

Hudut:

Hudut is a popular Garifuna dish prepared from mashed plantains (known as "machuca") and eaten with a coconut milk-based fish stew. The meal is a delectable blend of flavors, with the creamy coconut milk complimenting the tender fish and the subtle sweetness of the plantains. Many restaurants and hotels in Hopkins provide Hudut, and some even offer culinary workshops to teach you how to prepare this local delicacy.

Cassava Bread:

Cassava bread, known as "ereba" in the Garifuna language, is a staple of Garifuna cuisine. The bread is created by grating cassava root, drying it, and baking it into thin, crispy rounds. Cassava bread is commonly consumed with soups, stews, and as a snack. Cassava bread may be purchased in Hopkins from local bakeries or street vendors, and some cultural organizations provide demonstrations of the traditional bread-making process.

Darasa:

Darasa is another unique Garifuna cuisine, similar to tamales but made using shredded green bananas instead of corn masa. Bananas are combined with coconut milk and spices, then wrapped in banana leaves and baked. The result is a delightful and filling dish that is usually served as a side or snack. Darasa is less prevalent than other Garifuna cuisines, although it may be found at a few restaurants around Hopkins, especially during cultural events and festivals.

Sere:

Sere is a hearty Garifuna soup made with fish, coconut milk, and other vegetables such as yams, cassava, and plantains. The soup is thick and delicious, with the coconut milk giving a creamy smoothness and the vegetables adding a nice bite. Sere is typically served with cassava bread or rice, making it a filling and satisfying meal. Many local restaurants in Hopkins serve Sere, which is a must-try for those wishing to sample genuine Garifuna cuisine.

5.1.6 San Ignacio

San Ignacio, located in western Belize near the Guatemalan border, is both a gateway to the country's most important Maya archaeological sites and a popular adventure tourism destination. The town, located on the banks of the Macal River, is surrounded by lush forests, rolling hills, and ancient ruins, making it a perfect destination for both history fans and environment lovers. San Ignacio also has a diverse cultural past, including Creole, Mestizo, Maya, and Mennonite influences.

5.1.6.1 Maya Ruins and Archaeological Sites

San Ignacio is the best spot to experience Belize's rich Maya heritage, with numerous significant archeological sites within a short drive of the town.

Xunantunich:

Xunantunich, which means "Stone Woman" in the Maya language, is one of Belize's most impressive and well-preserved Maya ruins. The site is located on a hilltop overlooking the Mopan River, just a few kilometers from San Ignacio. The most distinctive feature of Xunantunich is "El Castillo," a 130-foot-tall pyramid that rises above the plaza. Climbing El Castillo's peak offers breathtaking views of the surrounding woodlands and the Guatemalan border.

The complex also includes numerous other temples, palaces, and plazas, as well as a small museum explaining the history and significance of Xunantunich.

Cahal Pech:

Cahal Pech, just a short walk from San Ignacio, is one of Belize's oldest Maya structures, with evidence of civilization reaching back to around 1200 BC. The site, which means "Place of Ticks" in the Maya language, was originally a prominent ceremonial center featuring plazas, temples, and residential structures. Cahal Pech is smaller and less frequented than the other Maya ruins in the vicinity, making it an excellent place to explore on your own. The site's modest museum gives information on Cahal Pech's history and the daily life of its people.

Caracol:

Caracol, Belize's largest and most important Maya site, is located deep within the Chiquibul Forest Reserve. The complex, which spans around 55 square miles, was once a strong city-state, rivaling Tikal in neighboring Guatemala. Caracol's most notable edifice is "Caana," or "Sky Palace," a massive pyramid that remains Belize's largest man-made structure. Other significant structures in the neighborhood include plazas, ball courts, and residential complexes. Caracol is less visited than other Maya sites due to its rural location, making it a great destination for anybody looking to escape off the beaten path.

The Actun Tunichil Muknal Cave:

The Actun Tunichil Muknal (ATM) Cave is one of Belize's most distinctive and intriguing archeological sites. The cave is located in the Tapir Mountain Nature Reserve and was utilized by the ancient Maya for ceremonial purposes, including human sacrifices. The cave is only accessible by guided tour, which requires walking through the forest, crossing rivers, and swimming into the cave's entrance. Visitors may explore a variety of things within, including pottery, stone tools, and skeletal remains, the most famous of which is the "Crystal Maiden," a young girl's calcified skeleton. The ATM Cave is a must-see for anybody interested in Mayan archeology or adventure.

5.1.6.2 Jungle and Nature Excursions

San Ignacio's location amid Belize's jungle makes it an excellent base for nature exploration, with a diverse range of activities available to outdoor enthusiasts.

Cave Tubing and River Exploration:

The rivers and caverns surrounding San Ignacio provide some of Belize's greatest options for adventure. Cave tubing, in particular, is a popular recreational activity that includes floating on an inner tube over a network of underground rivers and tunnels. The subterranean Branch River, which flows through a network of limestone tunnels, is the most popular cave tubing location. The adventure frequently includes a walk through the forest to the cave entrance, followed by a leisurely float into the dark, freezing passages. Throughout the journey, you will view breathtaking rock formations, stalactites, and stalagmites, as well as a variety of animals.

Mountain Pine Ridge Forest Reserve:

The Mountain Pine Ridge Forest Reserve, just a short drive from San Ignacio, is a magnificent expanse of pine forests, waterfalls, and rivers. The region is home to a variety of natural attractions, including the beautiful Rio River Pools, a series of cascading pools and waterfalls perfect for swimming and picnicking. The reserve also has the stunning Thousand Foot Falls, Central America's highest waterfall, and the Rio Frio Cave, a massive limestone cave with a wide aperture and a sandy riverbed. Hiking, bird watching, and animal spotting are popular activities in the Mountain Pine Ridge Forest Reserve, where the various ecosystems provide a home for a wide variety of animals.

Butterfly Farms and Botanical Gardens:

San Ignacio is home to various butterfly farms and botanical gardens where visitors may learn about the area's flora and animals. The Green Hills Butterfly Ranch, for example, is a working butterfly farm that breeds a wide variety of native butterfly species. Visitors may observe the whole butterfly life cycle, from egg to caterpillar to chrysalis to adult, while meandering through a lovely garden filled with hundreds of butterflies. The Belize Botanic Gardens, located just outside of San Ignacio, is another excellent resource for learning about the region's plant life. There are several themed gardens, such as an orchid house, a rainforest trail, and a medicinal plant garden.

Horseback Riding:

Horseback riding is a popular method to explore the countryside near San Ignacio, and various ranches and tour companies provide guided tours. Whether you're an expert rider or a beginner, horseback riding vacations provide a unique opportunity to view Belize's natural marvels. Rides frequently take you through woodland roads, along riverbanks, and to distant Maya sites, with several possibilities to see wildlife along the route. Some tours include a visit to a nearby hamlet, where you may learn about traditional farming methods and rural life in Belize.

Birdwatching:

Belize is a birdwatcher's dream, with over 500 identified bird species. Several bird species live in and around San Ignacio, including toucans, parrots, motmots, and kingfishers. The Macal River and the neighboring Elijio Panti National Park are excellent birding locations, with guided tours available for anyone interested in learning more about the local species. Whether you're an expert birder or a casual watcher, the diverse habitats surrounding San Ignacio provide several opportunities to see some of Belize's most magnificent and hidden species.

5.2 Must-See Attractions

Belize boasts a wide range of cultural, natural, and historical attractions to cater to a variety of interests. Belize provides a diverse range of activities, from ancient ruins to wildlife sanctuaries, making it a must-see Central American destination.

5.2.1 Great Blue Hole

The Great Blue Hole, located off the coast of Belize, is a world-renowned diving attraction and a UNESCO World Heritage Site. This massive marine sinkhole, about 300 meters wide and 125 meters deep, is a popular scuba diving and snorkeling spot. The deep blue waters offer a one-of-a-kind underwater experience thanks to its unique marine life, which includes reef sharks, gigantic groupers, and a large variety of tropical species. The beautiful Blue Hole is part of the Belize Barrier Reef Reserve System, the world's second-largest coral reef system, making it an excellent place for underwater study.

5.2.2 Belize Barrier Reef

The Belize Barrier Reef is a natural wonder that covers approximately 300 kilometers along Belize's coastline. It is home to a wide variety of aquatic animals, including vibrant corals, colorful fish, and endangered sea turtles. The reef is perfect for snorkeling and scuba diving, where tourists may explore coral gardens, underwater tunnels, and a diversity of marine life. The reef is separated into many zones, each offering a unique experience, ranging from shallow coral patches ideal for snorkeling to deeper spots suitable for professional diving.

5.2.3 Hol Chan Marine Reserve

Hol Chan Marine Reserve on Ambergris Caye is one of Belize's most popular snorkeling and diving destinations. The reserve is separated into four zones: coral reefs, seagrass meadows, mangroves, and Shark Ray Alley. Stingrays, moray eels, and tropical fish are among the marine animals that call the coral reef zone home. Shark Ray Alley, in particular, is well-known for its abundance of nurse sharks and southern stingrays, making for a thrilling snorkeling trip. The reserve's clear streams and well-preserved ecosystems make it a must-see destination for nature enthusiasts and explorers.

5.2.4 Belize Zoo

The Belize Zoo, located just outside of Belize City, is a one-of-a-kind wildlife preserve dedicated to the conservation and rehabilitation of native animals. The zoo is home to about 150 creatures from 45 Belizean species, including jaguars, tapirs, howler monkeys, and harpy eagles. Unlike other zoos, the Belize Zoo is built in a natural forest environment, with large enclosures designed to replicate the animals' natural habitats. The zoo allows visitors to observe and learn about Belize's animals up close, making it a popular destination for families and nature lovers.

5.2.5 Lamanai Archaeological Reserve

Lamanai, which translates as "Submerged Crocodile" in Maya, is one of Belize's most magnificent and significant Maya sites. Lamanai, located in the Orange Walk District, sits on the banks of the New River and provides a unique blend of archeological discoveries and natural beauty. The area is noted for its magnificent pyramids, particularly the High Temple, which provides panoramic views of the surrounding forest and river. Lamanai's secluded position in northern Belize adds to its attractiveness, with tourists typically coming by boat, enjoying the scenic ride through lush landscapes, and seeing wildlife along the route.

5.2.6 Cockscomb Basin Wildlife Sanctuary

The Cockscomb Basin Wildlife Sanctuary is one of Belize's most significant conservation zones, having created the world's first jaguar reserve. The sanctuary, which spans over 400 square kilometers of tropical forest, is home to a wide variety of creatures, including jaguars, ocelots, pumas, howler monkeys, and hundreds of bird species. The refuge offers a range of hiking paths, ranging from short treks to more demanding climbs that lead to spectacular landscapes and waterfalls. For birdwatchers, the sanctuary is a good spot to observe toucans, parrots, and other exotic species in their natural environment.

5.2.7 Barton Creek Cave

Barton Creek Cave, located in the Cayo District, is an ancient Maya ceremonial site and one of Belize's most accessible caverns. The cave is accessible via canoe, allowing tourists to glide through the chilly, dark waters while seeing the spectacular stalactites, stalagmites, and ancient Maya artifacts. The cave's chambers include pottery, stone tools, and bone remains, providing visitors with insight into the rites that took place over a thousand years ago. Barton Creek Cave blends adventure, history, and natural beauty, making it a must-see location for anybody interested in Maya culture or Belize's natural beauties.

5.3 Outdoor Activities

Belize is an outdoor enthusiast's dream, with a variety of activities that make use of the country's various environments, ranging from lush rainforests and towering mountains to beautiful beaches and coral reefs.

5.3.1 Hiking & Trekking

Belize's diversified landscape gives enough chances for hiking and trekking, with trails appropriate for all levels of expertise. The Mountain Pine Ridge Forest Reserve, which includes pine woods, waterfalls, and rivers, provides some of Belize's greatest hiking options. Trails such as the Rio on Pools and the Thousand Foot Falls provide breathtaking vistas and the opportunity to cool yourself in natural swimming holes. Another popular hiking site is the Cockscomb Basin Animal Sanctuary, which has pathways ranging from simple to challenging that lead to waterfalls, animal interactions, and panoramic vistas.

5.3.2 Snorkeling and Scuba-Diving

Belize is a famous snorkeling and scuba diving destination because of its Barrier Reef and other marine reserves. Hol Chan Marine Reserve and the Great Blue Hole provide some of the greatest underwater experiences in the world. Snorkelers may explore the vivid coral gardens and swim alongside schools of fish, while divers can descend to deeper waters to witness bigger marine species such as reef sharks, sea turtles, and rays. Snorkeling and diving in Belize is an exciting experience for both novice and expert divers, owing to the gorgeous seas and rich marine wildlife.

5.3.3 Kayaking or Canoeing

Belize's rivers, lagoons, and coastline are ideal for kayaking and canoeing. The Macal and Mopan Rivers in the Cayo District are good kayaking destinations, with the opportunity to spot wildlife such as iguanas, toucans, and howler monkeys along the way. Cave kayaking in Barton Creek Cave or the Caves Branch River is a more challenging excursion that includes paddling and exploring ancient Maya ceremonial sites. Coastal kayaking on Ambergris Caye and Placencia offers guests to explore mangrove forests, lagoons, and barrier islands, often seeing manatees, dolphins, and a variety of bird species.

5.3.4 Wildlife Watching

Belize's high biodiversity makes it an ideal place to observe animals. The Cockscomb Basin Wildlife Sanctuary is one of the greatest sites to watch jaguars in their native environment, although these secretive animals are rarely seen. However, the refuge is also home to many other species, such as howler monkeys, tapirs, and a variety of birds. Crooked Tree Wildlife Sanctuary is a birdwatcher's dream, especially during the dry season, when the lagoons attract large numbers of waterfowl, including the famous jabiru stork. Belize's rivers and coasts also provide opportunities to witness manatees, dolphins, and other marine animals, making wildlife viewing a popular activity across the country

5.3.5 Fishing

Belize is a world-renowned sport fishing destination, with coastal waterways, rivers, and lagoons filled with a wide variety of species. Fly fishermen flock to Belize to complete the "Grand Slam" of bonefish, tarpon, and permit all in one day. Ambergris Caye, Caye Caulker, and Placencia's flats are great for fly fishing, while deep-sea cruises let you capture bigger species including marlin, sailfish, and tuna. Whether you're an expert or a novice angler, Belize's rivers have something for everyone.

5.3.6 Zip-Line and Canopy Tours

Zip-lining through Belize's rainforest canopy is a memorable trip for adrenaline seekers. Several areas in the nation provide zip-lining activities, including the Bocawina Rainforest Resort and Caves Branch Adventure Company. These adventures frequently feature a succession of platforms and ropes that lift you into the trees, affording breathtaking vistas of the rainforest below. Some adventures involve rappelling down waterfalls or exploring tunnels, which adds to the thrill of the event.

5.3.7 Caving Adventures

Belize is home to some of Central America's most breathtaking caverns, many of which were utilized by the ancient Maya for ceremonies. In addition to Barton Creek Cave, the Actun Tunichil Muknal (ATM) Cave is a popular destination that provides a demanding and exciting experience. Exploring the ATM Cave, which is surrounded by ancient artifacts and bones, requires walking, swimming, and climbing through narrow passageways. The cave's chambers are packed with breathtaking rock formations and traces of Maya rites, making it an interesting destination for anybody interested in both history and natural beauty.

These outdoor activities represent only a small portion of what Belize has to offer. The country's diverse landscapes and ecosystems provide unlimited chances for discovery, adventure, and pleasure, making it a popular destination for all types of outdoor lovers.

6. Cultural Experiences

6.1 Local Culinary and Dining

6.1.1 Culinary Landscape

Belize's cuisine reflects its rich cultural diversity, incorporating ingredients from the Maya, Garifuna, Mestizo, Creole, East Indian, and other ethnic groups. This mix has resulted in a vibrant culinary environment as diverse as the people themselves. When visiting Belize, food lovers will discover a variety of tastes, ingredients, and culinary approaches that reflect the country's history, geography, and cultural traditions.

Staples of Belizean cuisine

Rice and Beans: Rice and beans are a common Belizean dish that can be found across the country. It consists of red kidney beans and rice cooked in coconut milk and is typically served with stewed chicken, pork, or beef and fried plantains. This meal reflects the influence of Creole cuisine and is a pleasant, flavorful dinner that every guest must enjoy.

Hudut: Hudut is a traditional Garifuna dish with marine elements in Belizean cuisine. It consists of mashed plantains (both ripe and green) served with a delicious coconut milk-based fish stew. The dish is frequently prepared with freshly caught fish, and the thick, creamy coconut broth is seasoned with herbs and spices to give it a distinct flavor.

Tamales: Tamales are a popular meal in Belize, particularly among Mestizo communities. They are made of masa (corn dough), loaded with meat, beans, or vegetables, then wrapped in banana leaves before steaming. Belizean tamales are often seasoned with a rich variety of spices, and the banana leaves provide a particular flavor to the dish.

Johnny cakes are a type of bread roll that is commonly eaten in Belize for breakfast or as a snack. Johnny cakes are an important element of Belizean cuisine. In addition to being frequently split open and filled with cheese, ham, or eggs, these baked pastries are generally prepared with flour, coconut milk, or baking powder. Johnny cakes are an essential component of Creole cuisine, known for their soft texture and somewhat sweet flavor.

Fry Jacks: Another popular morning dish in Belize, fry jacks resemble Johnny cakes in appearance. Deep-fried flatbread is commonly served with scrambled eggs, beans, and cheese. The dough bits are light and fluffy. They can be sweetened with honey, jam, or condensed milk, or eaten plain.

Escabeche is a chicken soup that is popular among Mestizo households owing to its delicious flavor. Its components include chicken, onions, and a broth seasoned with oregano, spices, and vinegar. The soup is often served with corn tortillas and is known for its sour and flavorful flavor.

Conch Fritters are a popular appetizer in Belize, especially along the coast and on the islands. Many individuals enjoy eating them every day. The fritters are made by blending chopped conch meat with flour, eggs, and a variety of seasonings, then deep-frying them till golden brown. They are typically served with a dipping sauce, and seafood lovers will enjoy the soft, somewhat chewy conch meat.

Salbutes are small, fried corn tortillas with a variety of toppings such as shredded chicken, lettuce, tomatoes, and pickled onions. They are a popular street food in Belize, often enjoyed as a quick snack or light meal.

Ceviche is a refreshing dish made from raw fish or seafood marinated in lime juice and served with onions, tomatoes, cilantro, and hot peppers. The acidity of the lime juice "cooks" the fish, creating a tangy, zesty dish ideal for enjoying in Belize's warm climate. Ceviche is a popular coastal food made with conch, shrimp, or fish.

Boil Up: Boil Up is a traditional Creole dish that combines a variety of ingredients in one pot. It frequently includes fish, eggs, pigtail, plantains, yams, cassava, and dumplings, all cooked together and served with a rich tomato sauce. This savory meal demonstrates the Creole community's resourcefulness and is a delicious example of Belizean comfort food.

Dining in Belize: What to Expect

Street Food: Street food is an integral part of Belizean culture, with some of the best local dishes available at roadside booths, marketplaces, and food vendors. Whether you're in Belize City, San Pedro, or any other town, you'll find a variety of street snacks that offer a taste of Belizean cuisine at a fair price. Tacos, tamales, pupusas, and empanadas are among the most popular street foods. These quick, delectable meals are ideal for folks on the go who want to experience authentic local food.

Restaurants and Eateries: Belize offers a wide range of dining options, from casual restaurants to premium businesses. Major cities and tourist destinations, such as San Pedro and Placencia, have a variety of restaurants serving both local and international cuisine. Seafood is especially plentiful along the sea, with several eateries serving meals made from freshly caught fish, lobster, and shrimp. Inland, more restaurants specialize in traditional Belizean cuisine, often with a focus on farm-to-table ingredients. Many establishments also cater to vegetarians and anyone with dietary restrictions, so you'll have no trouble finding a meal that suits your preferences.

Cultural Dining Experiences: To fully immerse yourself in Belizean culture, try attending a cultural dining event. Many communities, particularly Garifuna and Maya villages, offer guests the opportunity to learn about traditional culinary traditions and even help prepare a dinner. These experiences may include a demonstration of how to make foods like hudut or Maya chocolate, followed by a communal supper where you can enjoy the fruits of your labor. This is an excellent opportunity to meet locals, learn about their culinary traditions, and have a homemade Belizean supper.

Dining Etiquette: While dining in Belize is often a casual experience, there are a few standards to follow. It is customary for meals to be accompanied by lively conversation, and sharing food is a sign of hospitality. When dining in a local establishment, it is customary to sample a bit of everything served, even if it is only a small piece. In restaurants, tipping is encouraged but not compulsory; a 10-15% tip is considered generous. Belizeans have a strong appreciation for fresh, local ingredients, so don't be surprised if your supper takes a little longer to prepare—good food is worth the wait!

Must-Try Dining Destinations

Belize City, Belize's capital, offers a diverse range of dining options, from street food vendors to fine dining venues. Bird's Isle Restaurant, known for its seafood delicacies and waterfront views, and Nerie's II, a local favorite for Creole cuisine, are two must-visit establishments.

San Pedro, Ambergris Caye: San Pedro is a foodie's paradise, with a variety of restaurants serving everything from Belizean staples to international cuisine. Elvi's Kitchen is a popular spot for traditional Belizean cuisine, while Blue Water Grill serves seafood and sushi with a view of the Caribbean Sea.

Placencia: This seaside town is well-known for its superb seafood and informal dining options. The Secret Garden is a charming restaurant that serves Belize and Caribbean cuisine, whereas Rumfish y Vino is known for its imaginative, premium menu and extensive wine selection.

San Ignacio, located in the heart of the Cayo District, features a diverse culinary scene influenced by Maya, Creole, and Mestizo cultures. Ko-Ox Han Oh (Let's Go Eat) is a popular restaurant that serves traditional Belizean cuisine, whereas Guava Limb Café offers a farm-to-table dining experience with a focus on fresh, local ingredients.

6.2 Traditional Festivities and Events

Belize's calendar is jam-packed with vibrant festivals and events celebrating the country's rich cultural heritage, history, and traditions. These festivals provide travelers with a unique opportunity to experience Belizean culture firsthand, from the powerful rhythms of Garifuna drumming to the vibrant parades and dances of Carnival. Whether you're visiting for a huge national holiday or a tiny local celebration, Belize's festivals are sure to leave an impression.

6.2.1 Major National Festivals

Garifuna Settlement Day (November 19) is a major cultural festival in Belize that commemorates the landing of the Garifuna people on Belize's beaches in 1802. The day is celebrated with parades, drumming, dancing, and traditional Garifuna music, with the main activities taking place in Dangriga, Hopkins, and Punta Gorda. The celebrations typically begin the night before with drumming sessions and go until early in the morning. On the day itself, reenactments of the Garifuna's arrival in dugout canoes are followed by a full day of cultural events, including traditional dances such as the Jankunu and the Punta.

Belize Carnival (September): The Belize Carnival is a vibrant and colorful carnival held in September to honor the anniversary of the Battle of St. George's Caye and Belize's Independence Day. The Carnival is a highlight of the September festivities, including a colorful parade of people dressed in stunning costumes and dancing to the sounds of soca, calypso, and dancehall music. The parade moves through the streets of Belize City, gathering a large crowd. Carnival is a time of celebration, joy, and national pride, and it allows visitors to see Belizean culture in its most spectacular form.

September Celebrations: The whole month of September is a time of national pride and celebration in Belize, culminating in a series of festivities leading up to Independence Day on September 21. The celebrations start on September 10 with patriotic parades, flag-raising ceremonies, and cultural activities commemorating the

Battle of St. George's Caye anniversary. As Independence Day approaches, the celebrations intensify, with concerts, street gatherings, and fireworks shows. The celebrations culminate on September 21, with parades, formal events, and a general sense of excitement throughout the country.

Easter Celebrations: Easter is a significant religious occasion in Belize, celebrated with both solemnity and revelry. Easter weekend is celebrated with church services, processions, and many cultural festivities. Traditional Passion of Christ reenactments are held in the municipalities of Benque Viejo del Carmen and San Ignacio, attracting large crowds. One of Belize's most peculiar Easter traditions is the La Ruta Maya Belize River Challenge, a four-day canoe race down the Belize River that attracts racers from all over the world. The race is both a sporting event and a cultural celebration, with towns along the river turning out to cheer on the paddlers.

The Maya Deer Dance Festival (August) is a traditional ritual held in San Antonio, Cayo District. This festival is a prominent cultural event for Belize's Yucatec Maya community. The Deer Dance is a ceremonial dance that depicts the relationship between humans and nature, with participants dressed as hunters, deer, and other animals. The dance is performed to traditional Maya music on the feast day of St. Louis, the village's patron saint. The festival provides a rare opportunity to see an ancient Maya tradition that has been passed down through the generations.

Lobster Festivals (June-July): Belize's coastal communities celebrate the start of lobster season with lively lobster festivals in San Pedro, Caye Caulker, and Placencia. These events are a seafood lover's dream, with local restaurants and vendors serving up a variety of lobster specialties, including grilled lobster tails, ceviche, and lobster pizza. The festivals also feature live music, dance performances, and other contests, making them a fun and festive way to kick off the summer season.

Pan American Day (October 12): Pan American Day, also known as Columbus Day, is a public holiday in Belize commemorating the cultural diversity of the Americas. In Belize, the day is marked with cultural festivals, especially in Mestizo communities where it is also known as Día de la Raza. Celebrations include traditional dances, music, and parades, with an emphasis on the contributions of Belize's diverse ethnic populations.

Christmas and New Year's Celebrations: Christmas in Belize is a joyful time filled with cultural traditions and family reunions. The activities begin in early December with the lighting of Christmas trees and continue until New Year's Day. The Garifuna people conduct the Jankunu Dance, which is one of the most intriguing Christmas customs in Belize. Dancers dressed in colorful masks and costumes perform rhythmic dances to the beat of Garifuna drums, celebrating both the holiday season and their cultural heritage. On Christmas Eve and Day, families gather to eat traditional meals, exchange gifts, and attend church services. The New Year is celebrated with fireworks, parties, and a variety of cultural activities around the country.

6.2.2 Local and Regional Festivals

Toledo Cacao Festival (May): Held in Punta Gorda, the Toledo Cacao Festival commemorates Belize's rich chocolate-making heritage. The event offers a variety of activities, including chocolate-making demonstrations, tastings, and tours of local cacao farms. Visitors may learn about the Maya's historic cacao cultivation and processing traditions, as well as sample a variety of chocolates. The event includes cultural performances, live music, and a street market with local artisans and food vendors.

La Ruta Maya Belize River Challenge (March): As previously stated, the La Ruta Maya Belize River Challenge is an important event in Belize's cultural and sports calendar. The four-day canoe race from San Ignacio to Belize City includes 180 kilometers along the Belize River. The event is a test of endurance and ability, with teams paddling across a variety of conditions, including rapids, calm waters, and challenging twists and turns. The tournament draws

160

participants from Belize and other nations around the world, as well as spectators who line the riverbanks to cheer on the paddlers as they take to the water. During the marathon, villages along the course have celebrations with music, dancing, and food sellers. The race is more than simply an athletic event; it is also a cultural celebration.

Hopkins Mango Festival (June): The town of Hopkins, known for its vibrant Garifuna culture, hosts the annual Hopkins Mango Festival to commemorate the abundance of mangoes during the harvest season. The event features a variety of mango-inspired dishes, including mango salsa, mango smoothies, and mango treats, among others. In addition to the food selections, the event will feature cultural performances, live music, and children's activities. The Hopkins Mango Festival is a fun, family-friendly event that highlights the importance of agriculture and local goods in Belizean culture.

The San Pedro Lobster Festival (June) is a much-anticipated event on Ambergris Caye. It's a week-long festival that kicks off the lobster season. There will be a variety of events throughout the festival, including a lobster cook-off, beach parties, and a lobster crawl. During the lobster crawl, participants will visit various sites and sample lobster-themed foods and beverages. The celebrations culminate in a big block party including live music, dance acts, and fireworks. The San Pedro Lobster Festival is a vibrant and entertaining event that attracts both locals and tourists. It offers a unique opportunity to experience the island's culture and food.

Placencia Sidewalk Arts & Music Festival (February): This yearly festival celebrates the work of local artists, musicians, and craftspeople. The festival takes place along Placencia's famous promenade, the world's smallest main street. The event has art exhibits, live music performances, and artisan stalls where visitors may buy one-of-a-kind handcrafted items while also learning about Belizean culture. The festival also includes activities for children, making it a fun family event that celebrates the local community's creative spirit.

Belize International Film Festival (July): The Belize International Film Festival is a well-known event that brings together directors, actors, and film enthusiasts from across the world. The festival screens a wide range of films, including feature films, documentaries, and short films, with a focus on Caribbean and Central American cinema. The event includes screenings, panel discussions, and workshops, providing an opportunity for filmmakers to exhibit their work and engage with audiences. The Belize International Film Festival is a significant cultural event that promotes the growing film industry in Belize and the surrounding area.

6.3 Indigenous Culture and Communities

6.3.1 Maya People

The Maya civilization was one of the most important and long-lasting cultures in the Americas. Today, descendants of the ancient Maya people live in Belize, preserving their rich cultural heritage and practices. The Maya people of Belize are mostly concentrated in the southern districts of Toledo and Stann Creek, where they have preserved their language, customs, and way of life despite centuries of change.

Maya Communities in Belize

Toledo District: The Toledo District has the highest number of Maya communities in Belize, with cities like San Antonio, San Pedro Columbia, and Santa Cruz serving as cultural hubs for the Q'eqchi and Mopan Maya people. These villages are typically located in remote areas, surrounded by gorgeous woodlands and mountains, providing a glimpse into the old Maya way of life. Toledo's Maya people continue to practice subsistence farming, relying on old agricultural traditions including milpa, a type of slash-and-burn agriculture passed down through generations.

Stann Creek District: Maya settlements like Maya Centre and Red Bank are known for their strong cultural identity and ties to the land. These villages generally participate in eco-tourism projects, which allow travelers to firsthand experience Maya culture. This includes guided tours to ancient Maya sites, traditional culinary classes, and artisan workshops where guests may learn about Maya weaving, pottery, and basketry.

The Mayan Way of Life

Language and Oral Tradition: Language plays an important part in preserving Maya culture. The Q'eqchi and Mopan Maya languages are still spoken in many areas, and efforts are being made to guarantee that future generations may learn and speak their ancestral languages. Oral tradition is also an important part of Maya culture, with elders passing on stories, customs, and knowledge about the natural world to younger members of the community.

Spirituality and Religion: Maya spirituality is deeply rooted in the belief that all living things are inextricably linked and that the natural world has spiritual value. Many Maya tribes continue to practice traditional ceremonies and festivities that honor the land, the ancestors, and the Maya pantheon. Food, incense, and prayers are typically offered at these rites, which take place in sacred places such as caves, rivers, and mountains.

Agriculture and Food: Agriculture is fundamental to the Maya way of life, with many families relying on it as their primary source of income. Corn, beans, and squash, known as the "Three Sisters," are the fundamental crops of the Maya diet and are frequently grown together in a symbiotic relationship. The Maya also grow a wide range of fruits, vegetables, and medicinal plants, many of which are used in ancient culinary and therapeutic practices. The preparation of traditional foods such as tamales, maize tortillas, and cocoa-based drinks is an important cultural rite that connects the Maya to their ancestors and the environment.

Crafts and Artisanship: The Maya are known for their exceptional craftsmanship, particularly in the disciplines of weaving, pottery, and basketry. Maya women occasionally weave intricate textiles using backstrap looms, a process that has been passed down through centuries. These textiles are used to make traditional garments like huipils (blouses) and cortes (skirts), as well as ceremonial artifacts and household items. Pottery and basket-making are also important cultural heritage, with artisans creating beautiful, functional products used in daily life and festivities.

Visiting Maya Communities

Visitors to Maya communities in Belize are met with real friendliness, but these interactions must be approached with cultural awareness and respect. Here are some options for travelers who want to learn about Mayan culture:

Respecting Traditions: The Maya place a high value on their cultural traditions, and visitors should be aware of this when participating in cultural activities. This includes dressing modestly, obeying the instructions of local hosts, and refraining from photographing religious rites or sacred sites without permission.

Supporting Local Villages: When visiting Maya villages, consider supporting local businesses and craftspeople by purchasing handcrafted things, booking guided tours with local guides, and staying in community-run accommodations. This ensures that tourism benefits the local community and contributes to the preservation of Maya culture.

Learning with an Open Mind: The Maya have a rich and diversified culture, with a profound spiritual connection to the land and nature. Approach your visit with an open mind and eagerness to learn. Take the time to listen to the Maya people's stories and experiences, and respect the information that has been passed down for centuries.

6.3.2 The Garifuna People

The Garifuna people are another significant indigenous group in Belize, with a distinct cultural heritage that combines African, Caribbean, and Indigenous influences. The Garifuna community is mostly centered along Belize's southern coast, in towns such as Dangriga, Hopkins, and Punta Gorda. Their culture is designated by UNESCO as a Masterpiece of the Oral and Intangible Heritage of Humanity, demonstrating the richness and diversity of Garifuna practices.

Garifuna Community in Belize

Dangriga: Known as Belize's cultural heart, Dangriga is the country's largest Garifuna town. The town is a vibrant center of Garifuna culture, with a strong emphasis on music, dance, and the arts. Visitors to Dangriga can watch traditional Garifuna drumming and dance performances, visit cultural institutions and museums, and participate in classes that teach Garifuna drumming and cooking.

Hopkins: Hopkins is a smaller, more laid-back Garifuna village that offers a peaceful respite while maintaining a significant cultural presence. The neighborhood is known for its beautiful beaches, friendly population, and cultural immersion programs. Visitors can stay in guest houses run by Garifuna families, sample traditional Garifuna cuisine, and participate in cultural activities like cassava bread-making and Garifuna language training.

Punta Gorda is Belize's southernmost town and acts as a gateway to the Toledo District's vibrant cultural scene. The town is home to a substantial Garifuna community, and travelers may learn about Garifuna culture through music, dance, and cuisine. Punta Gorda is also an excellent place to visit the indigenous Maya villages and engage in ecotourism activities.

Garifuna Way of Life

Language and oral tradition: The Garifuna language is an important part of the community's identity, and efforts are being made to preserve and revitalize it among future generations. The language is a hybrid of Arawak, Carib, and African languages, with traces of Spanish and English. Oral tradition is an essential part of Garifuna culture, with stories, proverbs, and songs passed down through generations.

Music and dancing are central to Garifuna culture, with drumming playing an important role in both secular and spiritual activities. The ancient drums, known as "Segunda" and "Primera," are made of hollowed-out tree trunks and utilized to create the distinctive rhythms of Garifuna music. Popular Garifuna dances include the Punta, a loud dance with African roots, and the Jankunu, a ceremonial dance performed during Christmas and New Year's celebrations. The Garifuna's music and dance are powerful reflections of the community's history, struggles, and resilience.

Cuisine: Garifuna cuisine reflects the community's coastal lifestyle, with a strong emphasis on seafood and root vegetables. Some of the most well-known Garifuna cuisines are Hudut, a fish stew served with mashed plantains; Cassava Bread, a flatbread prepared from grated cassava; and Bundiga, a plantain and coconut soup. These cuisines are often made using traditional techniques and ingredients, with recipes passed down through generations.

Spirituality and Religion: Garifuna spirituality is a distinctive blend of African, Indigenous, and Catholic traditions. Ancestor worship is an important aspect of Garifuna's spiritual life, with rites and ceremonies performed to honor the spirits of the ancestors. These ceremonies typically include drumming, chanting, and food and drink offerings. The Dugu ceremony is one of the most important spiritual activities in Garifuna culture; it is a healing ritual performed to satisfy the ancestors and seek their guidance.

Visiting Garifuna Communities

As with Maya civilizations, visiting Garifuna communities necessitates cultural understanding and respect. Here are some options for travelers who want to learn about Garifuna culture.

Participating in Cultural Activities: Many Garifuna communities provide cultural immersion activities for visitors, such as drum lessons, cooking classes, and dance performances. These programs provide a unique opportunity to learn about Garifuna customs directly from community members. When participating in these activities, it is essential to follow your hosts' directions and respect their customs and traditions.

Supporting Local Artisans: The Garifuna are well-known for their artistic abilities, particularly in drumming and weaving arts. Consider purchasing homemade drums, clothing, or other items from local artisans to support the community and bring home a piece of Garifuna culture.

Learning about the Garifuna Struggle: The Garifuna people have a long history of tenacity and resistance in the face of adversity, including displacement and racism. Take the time to learn about the Garifuna people's history and hardships, and admire their courage and perseverance in allowing their culture to survive and thrive.

In conclusion, One of Belize's most intriguing features is its rich cultural tapestry, which provides visitors with a unique opportunity to interact with the diverse people who live here. Belize's cultural experiences, from ancient Maya rites to vibrant Garifuna rhythms, provide a look into a world in which history, heritage, and community are intricately linked. When visiting Belize, take the time to engage with the people, learn their stories, and immerse yourself in the cultural traditions that define this country. Whether you're sampling local cuisine, attending a traditional festival, or visiting an indigenous hamlet, the cultural experiences you have in Belize will leave an indelible impression and improve your vacation in ways you'll remember for years to come.

Wildlife and Nature

Belize is a nature lover's heaven, with an uncommon blend of habitats, plentiful species, and breathtaking natural beauty. The country is a natural wonderland, with the world-renowned Belize Barrier Reef, gorgeous national parks, and wildlife sanctuaries. This chapter highlights Belize's most notable natural features and provides essential information for visitors wishing to immerse themselves in the country's pristine environment.

7.1 The Belize Barrier Reef

The Belize Barrier Reef is one of the most well-known natural wonders in the Western Hemisphere, stretching for over 185 miles along Belize's coastline. It is part of the Mesoamerican Barrier Reef System, which is the world's second-largest coral reef system after Australia's Great Barrier Reef. The Belize Barrier Reef, a UNESCO World Heritage Site, is known for its amazing marine biodiversity, crystal-clear waters, and vibrant coral formations.

7.1.1 Exploring the Belize Barrier Reef

The Belize Barrier Reef is a one-of-a-kind marine exploration destination that offers a wide range of activities for snorkelers, divers, and marine enthusiasts.

Snorkeling: Snorkeling in the Belize Barrier Reef is a simple and enjoyable pastime with several world-class locations to visit. Popular destinations include the Hol Chan Marine Reserve, where snorkelers may witness a variety of marine life, including magnificent corals, tropical fish, and exquisite rays. Shark Ray Alley, located within the Hol Chan Marine Reserve, provides a unique opportunity to swim among harmless nurse sharks and southern stingrays in shallow, clear waters.

Scuba Diving: Belize is a prominent scuba diving destination, with the Belize Barrier Reef offering some of the most beautiful dive locations in the Caribbean. The Great Blue Hole, a massive marine sinkhole located on the Lighthouse Reef Atoll, is arguably Belize's most well-known diving attraction. It allows experienced divers to explore its deep blue depths, where stalactites and rare marine species may be found. Other popular diving sites are Turneffe Atoll and Glovers Reef Atoll, both of which provide a diverse range of underwater settings, from coral gardens to cliffs teeming with marine life.

Marine Life: The Belize Barrier Reef is home to a diverse range of marine organisms, including approximately 500 fish species, 65 coral types, and several invertebrates.

Notable residents include the West Indian manatee, which may often be observed feeding in the shallow seagrass meadows, as well as dolphins, sea turtles, and a variety of tropical fish. The reef also houses endangered species including the hawksbill turtle and the Nassau grouper.

Conservation efforts: The Belize Barrier Reef has faced significant environmental challenges, such as coral bleaching, overfishing, and the effects of climate change. Belize, on the other hand, has been at the forefront of marine conservation, with efforts underway to preserve its reef biodiversity. In 2018, Belize became the world's first government to impose an offshore oil drilling moratorium to protect its marine habitat. Additionally, marine reserves, no-take zones, and sustainable tourism practices have been introduced to ensure the reef's long-term health.

7.1.2 Tips for Visiting the Belize Barrier Reef

Consider a Responsible Tour Operator: When planning snorkeling or diving trips, look for tour operators who prioritize reef conservation and use best practices to reduce environmental harm. Look for operators who have been accredited by organizations such as the Belize Tourism Board (BTB) and the World Responsible Tourism Awards.

Practice Sustainable Tourism: As a tourist, you can help to save the reef by following sustainable tourism practices. Avoid touching or standing on the coral, since even minor contact may be harmful. Use reef-safe sunscreen that does not include hazardous chemicals such as oxybenzone or octinoxate, which can cause coral bleaching.

Respect aquatic Life: While exploring the reef, keep a respectful distance from aquatic life. Avoid following or bothering animals, and do not feed them, as this may disrupt their usual behavior and nutrition.

7.2 National Parks & Reserves

Belize is home to a huge network of national parks, wildlife sanctuaries, and nature reserves, each offering a distinct perspective on the country's many ecosystems. These protected areas provide critical habitat for animals, including many endangered and rare species, while also allowing visitors to experience Belize's natural beauty directly.

7.2.1 Belize's Notable National Parks

Cockscomb Basin Wildlife Refuge: Located in the southern Stann Creek District, the Cockscomb Basin Wildlife Sanctuary is perhaps best known as the world's first jaguar refuge. This sanctuary, which covers more than 150 square miles, is a vast expanse of tropical rainforest, mountains, and rivers that provide habitat for jaguars and other wildlife. Visitors to Cockscomb may explore a network of well-kept roads that wind through the jungle, allowing them to see a variety of wildlife such as howler monkeys, ocelots, peccaries, and over 300 species of birds. The refuge also includes Victoria Peak, Belize's second-highest peak, which offers difficult hikes and breathtaking views for anybody looking for an adventurous adventure.

The Mountain Pine Ridge Forest Reserve stands in stark contrast to the lush rainforests that blanket most of Belize. The Cayo District is known for its pine-covered hills, granite outcrops, and gorgeous waterfalls. The area is known for its natural beauty and outdoor leisure opportunities, such as hiking, birdwatching, and swimming. The Rio On Pools, a series of natural swimming pools and cascading waterfalls ideal for a refreshing dip are one of the reserve's most popular attractions. Another must-see destination is Big Rock Falls, a breathtaking cascade that plunges into a deep pool, creating an idyllic setting for swimming and picnicking.

Blue Hole National Park, located near the town of Belmopan, is named after its main feature, the inland Blue Hole, a sapphire-colored sinkhole fed by an underground river. The park offers a variety of activities, such as swimming in the Blue Hole, visiting the vast cave systems, and hiking through the surrounding forest. St. Herman's Cave, located within the park, is a popular destination for cave exploration and tubing. Visitors may explore the cave's amazing formations and learn about its historic significance as a ceremonial site for the ancient Maya.

Bacalar Chico National Park and Marine Reserve: Located on the northern tip of Ambergris Caye, Bacalar Chico is both a national park and a marine reserve, with a diverse range of terrestrial and marine environments. The park is a UNESCO World Heritage Site and is known for its diverse wildlife, including a variety of birds, mammals, and marine life. The location is also historically significant, as it contains ancient Maya temples and evidence of early Maya maritime enterprises. Bacalar Chico offers a variety of activities for nature lovers, including hiking, birdwatching, snorkeling, and diving.

7.2.2 Wildlife Sanctuary and Conservation Areas

Crooked Tree Wildlife Sanctuary, located in the Belize District, is a birdwatchers' paradise. The sanctuary has a network of wetlands, lagoons, and rivers that provide critical habitat for a variety of bird species, including the endangered Jabiru stork, the largest flying bird in the Americas. During the dry season, when water levels drop, the sanctuary's lagoons serve as a vital feeding ground for migrating birds, making it an ideal location for birdwatching. Crooked Tree, a village within the refuge, allows visitors to experience rural Belizean life while also participating in guided birding tours conducted by professional local guides.

Community Baboon Sanctuary, despite its name, is dedicated to the conservation of the black howler monkey, locally known as the "baboon." Located along the Belize River in the Belize District, this community-led initiative includes over 200 landowners who have pledged to protect the black howler monkey's habitat. The refuge has one of the healthiest populations of these primates in Belize, making it a popular destination for wildlife enthusiasts. Visitors to the sanctuary may take guided excursions into the forest to see black howler monkeys in their natural habitat and learn about the community's conservation efforts.

Shipstern Nature Reserve: Located in the northern Corozal District, the Shipstern Nature Reserve is a privately managed reserve with a diverse range of ecosystems such as tropical forest, savanna, and mangrove swamps. The reserve is home to a rich range of wildlife, including jaguars, pumas, and over 300 species of birds. Shipstern also includes one of Belize's few remaining sections of coastal forest, making it an important habitat for many animals. Visitors may explore the reserve's network of trails, see the butterfly aviary, and take guided tours to learn more about the area's unique flora and wildlife.

7.2.3 Conservation Initiatives and Challenges

Belize's national parks and reserves contribute significantly to the safeguarding of the country's natural heritage. However, these protected areas face a variety of challenges, including deforestation, illegal hunting, and the effects of climate change. To address these issues, Belize has implemented several conservation initiatives, including the establishment of protected areas, community-based conservation projects, and public awareness campaigns.

Community Involvement: Local communities lead many of Belize's conservation efforts, which are vital to the country's natural resource preservation. Community-based conservation projects, such as the Community Baboon Sanctuary and the Toledo Institute for Development and

Environment (TIDE), involve residents in the management and preservation of their natural surroundings. These initiatives help to ensure that conservation efforts are sustainable and that local communities benefit from the preservation of their natural heritage.

Protected Area Management: Belize's government and non-governmental organizations collaborate to preserve and protect the country's national parks and reserves. This includes monitoring animal populations, enforcing laws to prevent illegal activity, and conducting research to better understand the country's ecosystems. Protected area management also necessitates combining conservation and sustainable tourism so that visitors may enjoy Belize's natural beauty without harming the ecology.

Climate Change Adaptation: Climate change poses a significant threat to Belize's ecosystems, particularly coral reefs and coastal habitats. Rising sea temperatures, acidification of the water, and more frequent storms are all issues that Belize must address to preserve its natural heritage. The government is actively working to address these challenges through programs such as the Integrated Coastal Zone Management Plan, which aims to protect Belize's coastal and marine resources from the effects of climate change.

7.2.4 Tips for Visiting National Parks and Reserves

Prepare for the Weather: Belize's weather may be unpredictable, particularly during the rainy season. When visiting national parks and reserves, you should be prepared for changing weather conditions. Bring light, breathable clothing, sturdy hiking shoes, and a waterproof jacket. Don't forget sunscreen, insect repellant, and plenty of water to stay hydrated.

Respect Wildlife: When visiting Belize's natural areas, it is critical to respect the species and ecosystems. Avoid agitating the animals, keep a safe distance, and never feed or touch them. To help maintain the ecology, follow the instructions of park rangers and guides, as well as park rules and regulations

Leave No Trace: Practice responsible tourism by leaving no evidence of your presence. To reduce your impact on the ecology, pack out any rubbish, avoid hurting plants, and stick to allowed paths. By following these guidelines, you may help protect Belize's natural beauty for future generations.

7.3 Bird Watching and Wildlife Sanctuaries

Belize is a birdwatcher's paradise, with over 600 species of birds identified inside its borders. The country's many habitats, ranging from tropical rainforests to coastal marshes, provide excellent habitat for a diverse range of bird species, making it a popular destination for birdwatchers. In addition to its avian diversity, Belize is home to a plethora of wildlife sanctuaries, each offering unique opportunities to observe and learn about the country's wildlife.

7.3.1 Birdwatching Hotspots

- As previously stated, the **Crooked Tree Wildlife Sanctuary** is one of Belize's best birding locations. The sanctuary's wetlands attract a large number of waterbirds, including herons, egrets, and kingfishers. During the dry season, the sanctuary attracts migrating birds, allowing birdwatchers to see rare species like the Jabiru stork and the elusive Agami herons. Guided birding tours are available, led by local experts who can help visitors identify the many species found inside the sanctuary.

- **Belize Audubon Society Reserves:** The Belize Audubon Society manages several important birding locations, including the Half Moon Caye Natural Monument and Guanacaste National Park. Half

Moon Caye is most renowned for its red-footed booby colony, which is one of the largest in the Caribbean. Visitors to the caye may see these gorgeous birds nesting on the ziricote trees, with frigatebirds and other seabirds. Guanacaste National Park, located near Belmopan, offers a more accessible birding experience, with well-marked trails and a diverse range of resident and migratory bird species.

- **Mountain Pine Ridge Forest Reserve:** Another excellent location for birdwatching, particularly for those interested in recognizing forest-dwelling species. The reserve's pine woodlands and broad savannas are home to a variety of raptors, including the rare Orange-breasted falcon and Stygian owl. The reserve is also one of the best places in Belize to see the stunning Keel-billed toucan, Belize's national bird, as well as other species such as the Emerald toucanet and Blue-crowned motmot.

7.3.2 Wildlife Sanctuary and Nature Reserves

Monkey River Wildlife Sanctuary: Located in southern Belize, the Monkey River Wildlife Sanctuary is a lesser-known gem that offers an unforgettable wildlife experience. The refuge is located on the Monkey River, which flows through thick rainforest, providing habitat for a varied range of wildlife. Visitors may take guided boat tours along the river to see black howler monkeys, iguanas, crocodiles, and a variety of bird species. Monkey River is also a great place to explore traditional Belizean culture and eat fresh fish.

Hol Chan Marine Reserve: While most known for its marine life, the Hol Chan Marine Reserve also offers opportunities for birdwatching and wildlife observation. The reserve includes several islands and mangrove forests that provide critical breeding and feeding grounds for seabirds and shorebirds. The reserve's diverse marine ecosystem also supports manatees, dolphins, and sea turtles. Snorkeling and diving are the most popular activities here, but birdwatchers will also find much to enjoy.

Cockscomb Basin Wildlife Sanctuary: In addition to serving as a jaguar preserve, the Cockscomb Basin Wildlife Sanctuary is an excellent location for bird-watching and Wildlife observation. The sanctuary's many ecosystems, which vary from rainforest to riverine, support a diverse range of bird species, including toucans, parrots, and hummingbirds. Other animal species found on the reserve include tapirs, peccaries, and the elusive jaguar. Visitors may discover the sanctuary's rich biodiversity through guided hikes and birding outings.

7.3.3 Tips for Bird Watching and Wildlife Observation

- **Bring the right gear:** To have the best birding and wildlife observation experience, you must be equipped with the right equipment. Binoculars are essential for watching birds and other creatures from a distance, and a field guide to Belize's birds can help you identify the species you come across. A camera with a competent zoom lens is recommended for capturing the beauty of Belize's wildlife.

Be Patient and Quiet: Wildlife viewing requires patience and a keen sense of awareness. When exploring Belize's natural areas, walk slowly and quietly to prevent frightening wildlife. Early mornings and late afternoons are ideal for birdwatching since many species are more active during these times.

- **Respect Nature:** As always, when birding or watching wildlife, it is critical to respect the natural environment. Maintain a safe distance from animals, avoid destroying their habitats, and heed the advice of park rangers and guides. By practicing responsible wildlife observation, you can help ensure that Belize's natural beauty is conserved for future generations.

To sum up, Belize's amazing natural beauty and extensive biodiversity make it a paradise for environment lovers and animal enthusiasts. From the vibrant coral reefs of the Belize Barrier Reef to the lush rainforests and national parks, the country offers an unparalleled opportunity to interact with the natural environment. Whether you're exploring the depths of the Great Blue Hole, walking through jaguar territory in the Cockscomb Basin, or birdwatching in the wetlands of Crooked Tree, your experiences in Belize will leave you with a deep appreciation for the country's distinctive locations and the need to protect them. As you plan your trip to Belize, take the time to immerse yourself in the natural wonders that make this country so special. Remember to tread lightly, leaving only footprints and taking only memories.

8. Practical Tips for Travelers

Traveling to Belize is an amazing experience that includes everything from breathtaking natural landscapes to vibrant cultural encounters. To ensure that your trip is a success, you must plan ahead of time and be knowledgeable of what to expect and how to deal with the local environment. This section provides thorough information on practical considerations for travelers, such as packing fundamentals, local customs, communication options, and emergency contacts.

8.1 Packing Essentials

Packing carefully for your Belize holiday might make all the difference in your overall experience. Given Belize's diverse activities and climates, careful preparation is required.

8.1.1 What to Pack for Various Activities

Beach and Water Activities:

- **Swimwear:** Pack a variety of swimwear since you'll be spending a lot of time in the water.

- **Beach Towel:** While many accommodations provide towels, bringing your quick-drying beach towel might be handy.

- **Water Shoes:** Required for activities such as snorkeling or exploring the reef, where sharp corals and sea urchins may exist.

- **Snorkeling Gear:** While many trip operators provide gear, bringing your own ensures proper fit and comfort.

- **Sun Protection:** Wear a broad-brimmed hat, polarized sunglasses, and reef-safe sunscreen. The tropical sun is intense, and protecting your skin is critical.

- **Dry Bag:** Ideal for keeping valuables like your phone and camera dry during water-related activities.

Adventure and Hiking:

- **Sturdy Hiking Shoes:** Choose lightweight, breathable shoes with good grip. If you plan on visiting rainforests, bring waterproof clothes.

- Quick-dry shirts and trousers are ideal for humid conditions and strenuous activity.

- **Bug Repellent:** Mosquitoes and other insects are common, especially in forested areas. A good insect repellent is vital.

- **Reusable Water Bottle:** Staying hydrated is essential, especially while trekking. Many eco-lodges and parks feature refill stations, so bringing a reusable bottle is both handy and environmentally beneficial.

- **First-Aid Kit:** Include bandages, antiseptic wipes, blister pads, and any personal medicines.

- **Multi-tool or Swiss Army Knife:** Useful for a variety of tasks, such as cutting fruit or repairing gear.

- **Camera or binoculars:** Required for photographing Belize's amazing wildlife and breathtaking scenery.

City and Cultural Exploration:

- **Lightweight, comfortable clothing:** Breathable materials are ideal for the tropical climate. Casual yet modest attire is usually suitable in most situations.

- **Walking Shoes:** Comfortable shoes are vital for visiting cities, towns, and cultural sites.

- **Reusable Shopping Bag:** Ideal for carrying souvenirs, snacks, and beach essentials.

- **Guidebook and Map:** While cell phones are convenient, carrying a hardcopy guidebook or map might be useful in areas with limited internet access.

- **Portable Charger:** Keep your gadgets powered, especially after long days of touring.

8.1.2 Weather-appropriate Clothing

Belize has a tropical climate, which means it is warm all year with distinct wet and dry seasons. Packing the right gear is essential for comfort and functionality.

Dry Season (November-April):

- **Lightweight, breathable materials**: Cotton, linen, and moisture-wicking synthetic textiles are effective in keeping you cool in the heat.

- **Layering Pieces:** Evenings may be cool, especially inland or at higher elevations, so bring a lightweight jacket or sweater.

- **Sun Protection:** In addition to sunscreen, long-sleeved clothing and wide-brimmed hats may help shield you from the sun.

- **Rain Jacket or Poncho:** Although the dry season is often rain-free, unexpected showers may occur, particularly in forested areas.

Wet Season (May-October):

- **Rain Gear:** Bring a waterproof jacket or poncho. Clothing that dries quickly is essential during this time.

- **Umbrella:** A compact and easy-to-handle umbrella might be useful for dealing with rain.

- **Waterproof Footwear:** Consider shoes that can withstand muddy conditions, especially if you want to hike.

- **Spare clothes:** Due to increased humidity, clothes may take longer to dry, so carry a few spare outfits.

General Tips:

- **Laundry Services:** Many hotels and lodges provide laundry services, so you may travel less if you plan to wash laundry while on vacation.

- **Cultural Considerations:** While Belize is generally casual, it is normal to dress modestly while visiting cultural or religious sites.

8.2 Local Etiquette and Customs

Understanding and honoring local customs is essential for a memorable stay in Belize. While the country is known for its kind and welcoming citizens, being aware of social norms might help you conduct interactions more efficiently.

8.2.1 Social Norms and Practices

Greetings:

- **Friendly and informal:** Belizeans are known for their friendliness. A simple "Hello," "Good morning," or "Good afternoon" is customary and appreciated while interacting with natives.

- **Handshakes** are the most common way for men and women to meet one another, and they are typically accompanied by a smile. In more remote areas, welcomes may be more casual.

- **Titles and Respect:** It is customary to use titles such as Mr., Mrs., or Miss followed by the person's first name (e.g., "Mr. John") to show respect, especially when meeting someone for the first time.

Public Behavior:

- **Modesty:** Belizeans are generally modest, and although beachwear is OK on the beach, it is best to dress more modestly in cities and towns.

- Belize operates on "island time," which means a more relaxed attitude to punctuality. However, it is still polite to come on time for formal meetings or tours.

- **Conversations:** Belizeans like nice conversation and may make personal queries to get to know you. Engage generously, but you are not required to share more than you are comfortable with.

Photography

- **Permission:** Always obtain permission before photographing people, especially in indigenous or rural regions. Some locals may feel uncomfortable or want a little fee.

- **Respect Sacred Places:** Some cultural or religious sites may have restrictions on photography. Before shooting images, always check for signs or consult with a guide.

Dinner Etiquette:

- **Casual Atmosphere:** Dining in Belize is frequently informal and relaxed. Dress codes are lenient, even at many high-end establishments.

- **Shared Meals:** In a communal or family setting, it is customary to wait until everyone has been served before starting your meal.

- **No hurry:** Meals are meant to be enjoyed at a leisurely pace, so don't hurry out once you've finished eating.

8.2.2 Tips and Gratuities

Tipping practices in Belize may differ greatly from what you're used to, so it's important to understand local expectations.

Restaurants:

- The standard tip at restaurants is 10-15%. Some businesses may add a service charge to the bill, so check before tipping.

- **Casual Dining:** Tipping is optional at more casual cafés or street food vendors, although it is always appreciated if the service is outstanding.

Hotels and Lodges:

- Porters and cleaning people are often tipped BZ$1-2 for each bag and BZ$5-10 per night, depending on the level of service.

- **Guides:** For guided excursions, tipping your guide BZ$10-20 per person for a half-day tour and BZ$20-40 for a full-day tour is customary, depending on the quality of the experience.

Taxi and Transportation:

- **Taxis:** Tipping taxi drivers is optional, however rounding up the fare to the nearest dollar or leaving a little tip is appreciated.

- **Boat Captains and Crew:** For boat trips, especially those that include snorkeling or fishing, it is customary to tip the captain and crew BZ$10-20 per person, depending on the length of the trip and the quality of service.

Local Markets and Shops:

- **Artists and sellers:** Tipping is not necessary when purchasing from local markets or street vendors, however, if you get excellent service, a little tip or rounding up your purchase amount is appreciated.

General Tips:

- **Local Currency:** Tipping is usually done in Belize dollars (BZ$), however US dollars are sometimes accepted. If paying in US dollars, be sure the amount matches what you would tip in Belize dollars.

Carry tiny notes and coins for tipping, since change is not always available.

8.3 Internet & Communication

Staying connected while traveling in Belize is typically simple, although the availability and quality of service may differ depending on your location. Understanding the many options for mobile networks, SIM cards, and Wi-Fi availability may help you stay in touch with home and receive important travel information.

8.3.1: Mobile Networks and SIM Cards

Mobile Coverage:

- Belize has two principal mobile network providers: Belize Telemedia Limited (BTL), operating under

198

the DigiCell brand, and Smart. Both provide quite widespread coverage throughout the country, however service may be limited in remote or rural areas.

- **Metropolitan vs. Rural Areas:** Belize City, Belmopan, and San Pedro have excellent mobile coverage. In more remote locations, coverage may be limited or non-existent, particularly in dense forest regions or on small cays.

SIM Cards:

- **Traditional SIM Cards:** Travelers to Belize may get local SIM cards from major providers like DigiCell and Smart. SIM cards are widely available at airports, big cities, and numerous convenience stores. When applying for a SIM card, you must give your passport.

- **eSIM Availability:** Belize now accepts eSIM technology, which is a convenient option for travelers who own eSIM-compatible cell phones. eSIM allows you to activate a cellular plan without the need for a real SIM card, making it easier to stay connected without changing cards. eSIMs may be obtained online via the cell carriers' websites or apps, or you can go to a local store for assistance in setting it up.

How to Get an eSIM:

- **Online Purchase:** If your smartphone supports eSIM, you may buy and activate one via DigiCel or Smart's website. This may be done before your trip, allowing you to receive service the moment you arrive.

- **Local purchase:** If you want to buy your eSIM in Belize, go to a mobile provider's store. The staff can assist you with setting up the eSIM and selecting a data plan that matches your needs.

- **eSIM Activation:** After purchasing an eSIM, you will get a QR code or activation link. Scan the QR code or click the link on your eSIM-compatible smartphone to install the digital SIM and activate your cellular plan.

Prepaid Plans:

- Both DigiCell and Smart provide prepaid plans that include internet, phone, and text services. These plans may be topped up at a variety of retail locations or online. Consider a plan that can handle your data needs, especially if you expect to utilize maps, social media, or other data-intensive apps.

Mobile Data:

- **4G and 3G Networks:** Both major carriers provide 4G LTE in most urban areas, with 3G available in many rural areas. Data rates are usually acceptable for browsing, social networking, and video calls, however, they may slow down during peak hours or in rural areas.

- **Internet Cafes:** If you live in a smaller city or don't have a local SIM card, internet cafes are a great way to go online. These are becoming less common as Wi-Fi connectivity increases, although they may still be found in some areas.

8.3.2 Wi-Fi Availability

Hotels and Accommodations:

- Wi-Fi is often available at hotels, resorts, and lodges, however, the quality and speed may vary. Wi-Fi is often provided for free at high-end accommodations, including guest rooms and social areas. In low-cost motels, it may be limited to common areas or charge a minimal fee.

- Wi-Fi may only be available in limited places, such as the lobby or dining area, and may be slower than in urban areas. Some venues purposefully limit connectivity to enhance the "off-the-grid" experience.

Cafes and Restaurants:

- **Wi-Fi hotspots:** Many cafés and restaurants in tourist areas provide free Wi-Fi to customers. It is common to see signs indicating that Wi-Fi is available, or you may ask the staff for the password.

- **Expectations:** While Wi-Fi is normally free, it is courteous to pay if you intend to use it for an extended period. Some venues may limit the time you may use Wi-Fi, especially during peak hours.

Public WiFi:

- **Limited Availability:** Public Wi-Fi is less common in Belize than in other countries. However, it may be found in parks, city squares, or shopping districts in larger cities.

- **Security Considerations:** When using public Wi-Fi, be cautious about security. Avoid accessing sensitive information such as bank accounts or personal data across unsecured networks. Consider using a VPN (Virtual Private Network) to increase security.

Staying Connected:

- **Local SIM vs. Wi-Fi:** If you need to stay connected for business or personal reasons, a local SIM card with a data plan provides the most reliable connection, especially while traveling between many locations. Wi-Fi is ideal for casual use, although it may not be as reliable, particularly in rural or remote locations.

General Tips:

- **Downloading Maps and Information:** Before going to areas with limited internet access, download maps, travel guides, or vital information to your smartphone. This allows you to browse it offline, without relying on internet access.

- **Emergency Communication:** Make sure you have a way to communicate in case of an emergency. Have your phone charged, carry a portable power bank, and have important contact information both on your phone and written down in case of a battery failure.

8.4 Emergency Contacts

When traveling, it is critical to have emergency contact information and learn how to seek assistance. Tourists in Belize have various alternatives in the event of a crisis, including embassies, consulates, and local emergency services.

8.4.1 Embassy and Consulates

US Embassy:

The United States Embassy in Belize is located in Belmopan, the capital city. It offers several services to US residents, including passport renewal, notarial services, and crisis intervention.

Contact Information:

- **Address:** Floral Park Road, Belmopan, Cayo District, Belize

- **Phone:** +501-822-4011

- **Website:** United States Embassy in Belize

Canada High Commission:

Canada is represented in Belize via its High Commission in Guatemala, which is in charge of Belize. Canadians in need of diplomatic assistance may contact the Honorary Consulate in Belize City.

Contact Information:

- **Honorary Consulate Address:** 3 Cork Street, Belize City, Belize.

- **Phone:** +501-223-1060

- **Website:** Canada in Guatemala

British High Commission:

The British High Commission in Belize is located in Belmopan. It provides services to British residents such as emergency travel documents, consular assistance, and crisis response.

Contact Information:

- North Ring Road in Belmopan, Cayo District, Belize

- **Phone:** +501-822-2146

- **Website:** British High Commission Belize

Other Embassy and Consulates:

Belize has many other embassies and consulates, including those of Mexico, Guatemala, Taiwan, and Cuba. Travelers from these countries should contact their embassies for assistance.

General Tip: Before traveling, register with your embassy. This allows them to reach out to you in the event of an emergency, such as a natural disaster or political unrest.

8.4.2 Local Emergency Numbers

General Emergency Services:

- **911:** This is Belize's primary emergency number, used for police, fire, and medical emergencies. It is analogous to 911 in the United States and Canada.

- **Availability:** Emergency services are available across the country, however, response times may vary, especially in remote areas.

Police:

- **Tourist Police:** Belize maintains a special Tourist Police Unit (TPU) dedicated to ensuring the protection of visitors. They are often stationed at popular tourist destinations and may assist with situations such as lost things, safety concerns, and general inquiries.

- **Non-Emergency Call:** For non-emergency matters, contact your local police station. Police stations may be found in most towns and cities.

Medical Service:

- **Public Hospitals:** Belize has public hospitals in major towns such as Belize City, Belmopan, and San Ignacio. These hospitals provide emergency care, however, the facilities may be more basic than those in North America or Europe.

- **Private Clinics:** In tourist areas, private clinics provide more comprehensive treatment with shorter wait times. These institutions can handle minor emergencies, and many accept international health insurance.

- **Ambulance Services:** These services are available in large metropolitan areas. However, in remote areas, summoning an ambulance may take longer, so have a plan in place if you're involved in high-risk activities.

Fire Services:

- The Belize National Fire Service is in charge of fire emergencies. They have stations in major cities and towns, however, response times may vary in more remote areas.

Coast Guard:

- If you encounter an emergency while at sea, the Belize Coast Guard may be summoned for assistance. They are in charge of maritime safety and security and are prepared to lead rescue efforts.

General Tips:

- Prepare for an emergency by familiarizing yourself with the location of the nearest embassy, consulate, and medical facility upon arrival. Keep a list of important phone numbers on your phone and write them down in case your phone battery dies.

- **Vacation Insurance:** Make sure your vacation insurance covers emergency medical care, evacuation, and other scenarios. Keep your insurance information handy, as well as the phone numbers for your provider.

- **Local Contacts:** If you are staying in a remote area or participating in adventurous activities, notify someone of your plans and expected return time. This might be a hotel employee, tour guide, or companion.

8.5 LGBTQ+ Travel Tips

Belize is a wonderful and welcoming country, but like with any travel experience, it's important to be informed of local attitudes and policies regarding LGBTQ+ issues.

Legal Status and Social Attitudes:

- **Legal Protections:** In 2016, Belize decriminalized same-sex sexual behavior, marking a significant step forward for LGBTQ+ rights in the country. However, there are no legal protections against discrimination based on sexual orientation or gender identity.

- **Social Acceptance:** Belizean society is predominantly conservative, particularly in rural areas. While larger towns and tourist locations are more tolerant, public displays of affection by same-sex couples may attract unwanted attention. Discretion is advised, especially in less frequented spots.

LGBTQ+-Friendly Spaces:

- **Accommodations:** Some hotels and resorts in Belize are LGBTQ+-friendly, particularly in popular tourist destinations such as San Pedro and Placencia. It's a good idea to research and choose accommodations that are known to be welcoming to LGBTQ+ visitors.

- **Social Venues:** While Belize lacks a vibrant LGBTQ+ nightlife culture, there are bars and clubs in Belize City and San Pedro where LGBTQ+ visitors may feel more comfortable. These establishments may not be exclusively LGBTQ+, but they are often accepting and inviting.

Health & Safety:

- **Healthcare:** LGBTQ+ travelers should have no problem accessing healthcare services in Belize.

However, it is suggested that those seeking specialist medical therapy related to gender identity plan ahead of time since specialized alternatives may be limited.

- **Travel Insurance:** Make sure your travel insurance covers LGBTQ+-specific issues, such as emergency medical treatment and other unexpected events that may arise during your trip.

Cultural Respect:

- Local community engagement requires a polite and culturally aware approach. Understanding that Belize is still on the path to full acceptance may help LGBTQ+ visitors approach their interactions with compassion and caution.

- **Tourist Police:** The Tourist Police Unit (TPU) in Belize is trained to assist all tourists, including LGBTQ+ visitors. If you encounter any difficulties, they can assist and ensure your safety.

Finally, traveling in Belize offers a diverse range of experiences, from cultural encounters to natural wonders. You may ensure a safe and enjoyable trip by properly planning ahead of time, adhering to local customs, being connected, and knowing how to seek assistance in an emergency. Preparation is essential for making the most of your trip in this beautiful country, so plan ahead of time and travel responsibly.

Sustainable and Responsible Tourism

Sustainability and ethical tourism have become critical components of the modern travel experience, especially in a country like Belize, where natural beauty and biodiversity are major draws. Visitors to Belize are encouraged to engage in acts that protect the environment, assist local people, and ensure that the impact of tourism is positive and sustainable. This section provides a comprehensive overview of Belize's ecotourism initiatives, conservation projects, and practical tips for responsible travel.

9.1 Ecotourism Initiatives

Belize was a pioneer in ecotourism, emphasizing early on the need to protect its natural resources and encourage sustainable travel. Ecotourism in Belize focuses on enabling visitors to discover the country's diverse ecosystems while minimizing their environmental impact.

Protected Areas and National Parks:

- **Marine Reserves:** Belize has many marine reserves, including the Hol Chan Marine Reserve, South Water Caye Marine Reserve, and Glover's Reef

Marine Reserve. These areas are critical to the survival of marine life, such as coral reefs, fish species, and sea turtles. Visitors may engage in activities like snorkeling, diving, and wildlife observation while supporting conservation efforts via entry fees and guided tours.

- **Terrestrial Protected Areas:** Belize has many national parks and natural reserves, including the Cockscomb Basin Wildlife Sanctuary, which houses the world's first jaguar preserve, and the Mountain Pine Ridge Forest Reserve, which is known for its unique pine forest setting. These protected areas are managed by both government agencies and non-governmental organizations (NGOs), and they play an important role in preserving Belize's terrestrial biodiversity.

Sustainable Lodging:

- **Eco-Lodges:** Belize offers a variety of eco-lodges that are designed to have little environmental impact. These motels use sustainable building materials, renewable energy sources, and water-saving methods. Many eco-lodges engage in community-based tourism, which allows guests to learn about local cultures while simultaneously contributing to community development efforts.

Green Certifications: Some Belize accommodations have received certifications such as Green Globe or Rainforest Alliance Verified, demonstrating their commitment to sustainable operations. Choosing authorized hotels ensures that your stay benefits the environment and local communities.

Community-Based Tourism:

- **Cultural Tours:** Community-based tourism in Belize allows visitors to engage with local cultures in a respectful and meaningful way. Cultural excursions in Maya villages, for example, provide insight into traditional activities like cacao manufacturing, weaving, and farming. These trips are often led by community members, ensuring that the economic benefits of tourism stay within the community.

- **Local Handicrafts:** Buying directly from local craftspeople helps to preserve traditional crafts while also providing income for local households. Handwoven baskets, pottery, and natural jewelry are among the most popular items.

Wildlife Friendly Tourism:

- **Ethical Wildlife Viewing:** Belize's rich biodiversity offers a diverse range of birds, mammals, and marine life. Ethical wildlife viewing techniques are required to ensure that these species are neither disturbed nor damaged by humans. This includes adhering to recommended safe distances, avoiding feeding animals, and selecting tour operators that support wildlife conservation.

- **Support for Sanctuaries:** Visiting wildlife sanctuaries and rehabilitation facilities, such as the Belize Zoo or the Belize Bird Rescue, not only allows you to watch local wildlife up close but also contributes to the important work that these organizations do in rescuing and rehabilitating animals.

9.2 Conservation Projects

Belize is actively involved in various conservation activities to safeguard its unique landscapes and fauna. These projects often rely on collaboration among government agencies, non-governmental organizations (NGOs), local communities, and international partners. Travelers may support these projects by participating in volunteer programs or making donations and practicing responsible tourism.

Marine Conservation:

- **Belize Barrier Reef Reserve System:** The Belize Barrier Reef, a UNESCO World Heritage site, is the world's second-biggest coral reef system. It is home to an incredible diversity of marine life, including endangered species like the West Indian manatee and several sea turtles. Conservation efforts are focused on protecting the reef from threats like overfishing, coastal development, and climate change. Organizations such as the Belize Audubon Society and Oceana Belize are actively involved in these programs, providing opportunities for visitors to learn about and support reef conservation.

- **Coral Reef Restoration:** Coral reef restoration activities in Belize include the establishment of coral nurseries and the transplantation of healthy corals back into the reef. These activities are critical for mitigating the effects of coral bleaching and other environmental pressures. Visitors may participate in citizen science programs that monitor reef health and coral growth.

Terrestrial Conservation:

1. **Jaguar Conservation:** The Cockscomb Basin Wildlife Sanctuary is well-known for its jaguar conservation efforts. This sanctuary, established in the 1980s, protects a considerable number of jaguars in their natural habitat. Conservation programs include research on jaguar behavior, habitat protection, and strategies to reduce human-wildlife conflict. Visitors may help support the refuge by paying admission fees, making donations, and participating in educational programs.

- **Reforestation Projects:** Belize's reforestation projects aim to rehabilitate damaged forest areas, particularly those affected by logging or agricultural expansion. These projects usually involve the planting of native tree species, which helps to restore ecosystems and provides habitat for wildlife. Tourists may participate in tree-planting activities organized by conservation groups or volunteer their time to help with existing reforestation efforts.

Biodiversity Monitoring:

- **Citizen scientific efforts:** Belize offers a variety of citizen scientific programs in which travelers may actively participate in biodiversity monitoring. For example, the Belize Raptor Research Institute conducts bird monitoring and migratory studies, in which volunteers may assist with data collection. Similarly, marine research initiatives often include tourists in monitoring fish populations, coral health, and sea turtle nesting activity.

- **Wildlife Rehabilitation Facilities:** Supporting wildlife rehabilitation facilities such as the Belize Wildlife and Referral Clinic ensures that injured or orphaned animals get the care they need. Visitors may take guided tours of these facilities, learn about the challenges that affect Belize's wildlife, and contribute to their conservation efforts.

9.3 Responsible Travel Tips

Responsible travel is making informed choices that reduce the negative impacts on the environment and local people while maximizing the benefits of tourism. In Belize, where natural and cultural resources are an integral part of the holiday experience, practicing responsible travel habits is critical.

9.3.1 Reduce Your Environmental Impact

Minimizing Waste:

- **Limit Single-Use Plastics:** Belize has taken steps to reduce plastic pollution by banning single-use plastics such as plastic bags, straws, and Styrofoam containers. Travelers may give by bringing reusable items like water bottles, shopping bags, and silverware. Many hotels and restaurants in Belize support this movement by providing biodegradable or recyclable containers.

- **Waste Disposal:** Always dispose of trash correctly, particularly in natural areas. While hiking or visiting beaches, carry a small trash bag and dispose of garbage in designated containers. Participating in local clean-up programs is another method to help keep Belize's natural areas clean.

Conserving Water and Energy:

- **Water Conservation:** Water is an essential resource in Belize, especially in rural areas and islands. Travelers may save water by taking shorter showers, reusing towels, and turning off taps while not in use. Rainwater collection systems are used in certain eco-lodges, making conservation even more important.

- Energy efficiency is another way to reduce your environmental impact. Turn off lights, air conditioning, and equipment that are not in use. Many environmentally friendly accommodations in Belize use solar power and energy-efficient technology, but visitors still need to be mindful of their energy use.

Sustainable Transportation:

- **Public Transportation:** Using public transportation, such as buses or water taxis, may reduce your carbon footprint. Belize's public transportation system is stable and offers a true method to see the country while minimizing environmental impact.

- **Eco-Friendly Travel Options:** Biking, walking, and kayaking are excellent ways to see Belize's natural beauty without contributing to pollution. Many sights, especially on the islands, are easily accessible by foot or bike, and renting a bike or kayak might be a fun and environmentally friendly way to get about.

9.3.2 Supporting Local Communities

Respecting Local Culture:

- Belize is home to a variety of cultural groups, including Maya, Garifuna, Creole, and Mestizo. Travelers should appreciate these traditions and have an open mind. This includes seeking permission before photographing people or their property, learning about local customs, and participating in cultural activities respectfully.

- **Language and Communication:** While English is Belize's official language, learning a few words in indigenous languages like Kriol or Garifuna may help you connect with the people. It shows respect and interest in the local culture.

Supporting Local Businesses:

- **Shop Locally:** Purchasing goods and services from local businesses keeps money in the community and improves the lives of Belizean families. This includes eating at locally-owned restaurants, purchasing presents from local craftsmen, and hiring local tour guides.

- **Stay in Locally Owned Accommodations:** Choosing to stay in locally owned hotels, guesthouses, or eco-lodges rather than international chains ensures that your money directly benefits Belizean communities. Many local motels also support community development and environmental initiatives.

Volunteering and Giving Back:

- **Responsible Volunteering:** If you decide to volunteer during your stay, look for reputable organizations that address genuine community needs and have a positive impact. Avoid "voluntourism" that harms the local community or wildlife. Look for projects that align with your skills and allow you to make a meaningful difference.

- **Charitable Donations:** Another method to give back is to support local charities and NGOs that work in education, healthcare, conservation, and community development. However, do your study to ensure that your donations are going to reputable organizations that use funds wisely.

Ethical Wildlife Interactions:

- **Avoid Exploitative Practices:** Be wary of attractions that exploit nature, such as keeping or feeding wild animals for entertainment. Instead, consider visiting approved wildlife sanctuaries or taking eco-tours that support animal welfare.

- **Supporting conservation initiatives:** Contributing to wildlife conservation operations by donations, volunteer labor, or just choosing ethical tour operators may have a long-term impact on Belize's unique biodiversity. Look for trips and activities that have received certification or recommendations from conservation organizations.

Participate in Conservation Activities:

- **Eco-Tourism Tours:** In Belize, several tour companies provide eco-tourism experiences that combine adventure with conservation education. For example, you may go on a guided trip in a protected area where the guide highlights the importance of biodiversity and conservation efforts in the area.

- **Citizen Science Opportunities:** Certain conservation programs allow visitors to participate in data collection, monitoring, or research activities. This hands-on activity may enhance your vacation and contribute to ongoing conservation efforts in Belize.

Leave No Trace Principles:

- **Respect Wildlife and Nature:** Always follow the "Leave No Trace" guidelines while exploring natural areas. This includes staying on designated paths, avoiding plucking flora or disturbing animals, and leaving natural things and artifacts where they are found.

- **Responsible Snorkeling and Diving:** Belize's coral reefs and marine life are much endangered. When snorkeling or diving, avoid touching corals, cease feeding fish, and be mindful of your activities to avoid harming the underwater environment. To minimize your impact on the reef, always follow your dive or snorkel operator's advice.

In conclusion, sustainability and responsible tourism are critical to preserving Belize's natural beauty and cultural past. By adhering to these guidelines, travelers may ensure that their visit has a positive and long-term impact on the environment and locals. Responsible tourism is more than just limiting negative repercussions; it is also about actively contributing to the well-being of the places we visit, so that future generations may enjoy Belize's beauty.

Additional Tips and Resources

This section provides travelers with additional ideas, resources, and suggested itineraries that may help them plan a vacation to Belize. Whether you're a solo traveler, a family, a backpacker, a honeymooner, or an outdoor enthusiast, this book provides essential information to ensure that your trip is as smooth, enjoyable, and gratifying as possible.

10.1 Official Tourist Websites

Official tourism websites are excellent sources for current and accurate information on Belize. These websites, which are managed by government officials or official tourism organizations, include information ranging from visa requirements and travel warnings to detailed information on locations, accommodations, and activities.

Belize Tourism Board (BTB):

- The official website of the Belize Tourism Board is the primary source of information on all aspects of Belize tourism. It provides thorough information on sites, activities, hotels, and trip planning. The website also includes detailed travel warnings, safety tips, and up-to-date information on entry requirements. It is an invaluable resource for any traveler planning a trip to Belize.

- **Website:** https://www.travelbelize.org/

Belize Hotel Association:

- The Belize Hotel Association's website is an excellent resource for finding hotels in Belize. It lists a wide range of hotels, resorts, guesthouses, and eco-lodges, along with descriptions, photographs, and contact information. The website also provides information about special pricing and vacation packages.

- **Website:** https://www.belizehotels.org/

Belize Audubon Society:

- For travelers interested in ecology and conservation, the Belize Audubon Society's website is an invaluable resource. It provides detailed information on Belize's protected areas, such as national parks, wildlife sanctuaries, and marine reserves. The website also guides birdwatching and other wildlife-related activities.

- **Website:** https://belizeaudubon.org/

Belize Tourism Industry Association (BITIA):

- The BITIA's website has a wealth of information on Belize's tourism industry, including directories of tour operators, guides, and other travel services. It's an excellent website for anyone looking to book tours, excursions, and transportation in Belize.

- **Website:** https://www.btia.org/

Ministry of Health and Wellness:

Staying up to date on health standards and criteria is critical in today's global environment. The Ministry of Health and Wellness provides travel-related health information, vaccination requirements, and updates on potential health risks in Belize. Visit health.gov.bz.

These official websites provide travelers with reliable information directly from the source, ensuring that your travel plans are based on the most recent and accurate data available.

10. 2 Travel Apps

In today's digital age, travel apps are essential tools for making visiting a new location easier and more enjoyable.

The following are some significant apps that might enhance your travel experience in Belize:

Google Maps: A must-have for experiencing Belize, whether you're walking about Belize City, driving to the Maya ruins, or kayaking among the Cayes. Google Maps provides accurate maps, real-time traffic information, and directions. To avoid connectivity issues in remote locations, download maps offline ahead of time.

Maps.me: For those venturing off the beaten path, Maps.me is a viable alternative to Google Maps, offering exact offline maps. This application is particularly useful for hiking trails and rural areas where internet connectivity may be limited.

TripAdvisor: This app provides traveler reviews, photographs, and recommendations for various attractions, hotels, and restaurants in Belize. It's an excellent tool for finding highly rated activities while avoiding potential concerns.

XE Currency: Managing your budget while traveling is critical, and XE Currency provides accurate exchange rates, so you always know how much you're spending. Rates may also be obtained offline, making it useful in areas without an internet connection.

Duolingo: While English is Belize's official language, learning a few words in Spanish, Kriol, or Garifuna might enhance your tourist experience. Duolingo is a fun and easy-to-use language learning tool that offers lessons in several languages, allowing you to communicate more effectively with natives.

Belize Travel Health: This app provides health and safety information specific to travelers in Belize, such as clinic locations, safety tips, and updates on any health advisories.

Reef Smart Guides: If you want to dive or snorkel, this app provides detailed information on dive sites, including underwater maps and marine life identification. It is an essential tool for making the most of Belize's underwater attractions.

When used together, these tools may significantly enhance your travel experience, covering anything from navigation and language assistance to health advice and money management.

10.3 Itinerary suggestions

Creating an itinerary based on your travel style may enhance your experience in Belize. Whether you like solo adventures, family vacations, backpacking expeditions, romantic getaways, or outdoor explorations, these itinerary options provide flexible and diverse options to help you plan your trip.

For Solo Travelers

Day 1–2: Belize City and Surroundings

- **Explore Belize City:** Begin your tour by visiting the Museum of Belize, where you can learn about the country's history and culture. Wander around the Old Belize Cultural and Historical Center to gain a taste of Belize's rich history.

- **Day Trip to the Belize Zoo:** Located just outside the city, the Belize Zoo provides a unique opportunity to see native animals in their natural habitats. Continue with a boat ride along the Belize River to see wildlife including howler monkeys and crocodiles.

Day 3–4: San Ignacio and Cayo District

- **Discover Maya Ruins:** Head to San Ignacio, the gateway of Belize's historic riches. Visit Xunantunich, a magnificent Maya site, and then visit the lesser-known Cahal Pech ruin. These ancient cities provide a glimpse into the region's rich history.

- **ATM Cave tour:** Take a guided tour of the Actun Tunichil Muknal (ATM) Cave, where you'll hike, swim, and explore chambers filled with ancient Maya artifacts and skeletal remains.

Day 5–6: Caye Caulker

- **Relax on Caye Caulker:** After the excitement of the jungle, unwind on the tranquil island of Caye Caulker. Spend your days snorkeling at the Hol Chan Marine Reserve and Shark Ray Alley, or just relax at The Split, a popular sunset viewing location.

For Families

Day 1–3: Ambergris Caye

- **Stay in San Pedro:** Start your family vacation in Ambergris Caye, where you may enjoy water activities like snorkeling and swimming. Secret Beach is an excellent place for children to swim safely, and the Belize Chocolate Company serves delectable treats for all ages.

- **Marine Adventures:** Take a glass-bottom boat trip to see the stunning coral and marine life, or go on a family-friendly snorkeling excursion to the barrier reef.

Day 4–5: Belize Zoo and Cave Tubing

- **Visit the Belize Zoo:** Spend the morning visiting the Belize Zoo, which is known for its wildlife conservation efforts and fascinating animal shows. It is a fun and educational program for both children and adults.

- **Cave Tubing Trip:** Visit Caves Branch for a family-friendly cave tubing adventure. Float down the river through breathtaking limestone caves while learning about the natural and cultural history along the way.

Day 6–7: Placencia

- **Beach Time in Placencia:** Finish your tour on the sandy beaches of Placencia, where quiet waves provide ideal swimming conditions. Take a boat excursion to nearby islands or browse the local handcrafted shops in Placencia Village.

For Backpackers

Day 1–2: Caye Caulker

- **Backpacker vibe:** Begin your vacation on the budget-friendly island of Caye Caulker. The island's relaxed atmosphere, affordable accommodation, and bustling population of fellow travelers make it an ideal place to unwind.

- **Snorkeling and Exploring:** Rent a bike to explore the island, go on a group snorkeling adventure, or try your hand at paddleboarding.

Day 3–4: Hopkins and Garifuna Culture

- **Cultural Immersion:** Visit Hopkins, a village known for its rich Garifuna culture. Participate in a drumming session, sample traditional Garifuna cuisine, and enjoy the village's relaxed pace.

- **Outdoor Activities:** Kayak across the surrounding Sittee River or take a guided tour of the Cockscomb Basin Wildlife Sanctuary, which is home to jaguars and other wildlife.

Day 5–7: San Ignacio and the ATM Cave

Stay at a local hostel and explore San Ignacio, Belize's adventure capital. Visit the Maya ruins of Xunantunich, climb to the Rio On Pools, and don't miss the ATM Cave for a fascinating exploration of Belize's underground riches.

For Honeymooners

Day 1–3: Ambergris Caye

- **Romantic Getaway:** Begin your honeymoon on the beautiful Ambergris Caye. Stay at a beachfront resort, dine at luxury waterfront restaurants, and take a sunset cruise around the coast.

- **Snorkeling and Relaxation:** Spend your days snorkeling at the Great Blue Hole or getting a couple's massage at a nearby spa.

Day 4–5: Placencia

- **Beachfront Bliss:** Continue your honeymoon at Placencia, where you may relax on the beach, eat delicious seafood, and explore the surrounding coral cayes. A private boat tour or a visit to the Silk Cayes Marine Reserve makes for an excellent day out.

- **Romantic Dinners:** Enjoy romantic meals at coastal restaurants, and plan a night out at the Placencia Beach Club for cocktails under the stars.

Day 6–7: Mountain Pine Ridge

- **Nature Retreat:** End your honeymoon with a trip to the Mountain Pine Ridge Forest Reserve. Enjoy the peace and quiet of the forest, see the breathtaking Thousand Foot Falls, and have a guided tour of the Rio Frio Cave.

For Outdoor Enthusiasts

Day 1–2: San Ignacio and Cayo District

- **Maya Ruins & Hiking:** Begin your journey at San Ignacio, where you may see the ancient Maya city of Caracol, climb in the Mountain Pine Ridge Forest Reserve, and paddle along the Macal River.

- **Outdoor Activities:** The Cayo District offers a wide range of outdoor activities, including bird watching, horseback riding, and exploring natural lakes and waterfalls.

Day 3–4: ATM Cave Tour

- **Cave Exploration:** Join a guided tour of the ATM Cave, an exhilarating adventure that includes walking through the jungle, swimming across rivers, and viewing one of Belize's most significant archeological sites.

Day 5 to 7: Belize Barrier Reef and Lighthouse Reef

- **Diving and Snorkeling:** Spend the rest of your vacation exploring the Belize Barrier Reef, one of the world's top diving and snorkeling destinations. Take a dive excursion to the Great Blue Hole, a world-renowned underwater sinkhole, and Lighthouse Reef for some of Belize's best underwater sights.

10.4 FAQs

Q. When is the best time to visit Belize?

A: The best time to visit Belize is during the dry season, which runs from late November to mid-April. This month offers ideal weather for outdoor activities and viewing the country's attractions. The shoulder seasons (May to June and September to October) also provide wonderful weather, less people, and lower expenses.

Q. Do I need a visa to visit Belize?

A: Most countries, including the United States, Canada, the United Kingdom, and the European Union, do not need a visa for short-term travels (up to 30 days) to Belize. Tourists should, however, ensure that their passport is valid for at least six months beyond their expected departure date.

Q: What is Belize's currency, and may I use US dollars?

A: Belize's official currency is the Belize Dollar (BZD), which is pegged to the US Dollar at a set rate of two BZD to one USD. US dollars are widely accepted across the country, and prices are frequently quoted in both currencies. It is a good idea to carry small amounts of cash for convenience.

Q: Is Belize a safe destination?

A: Belize is generally a safe location, but visitors should take standard precautions such as avoiding isolated places at night, securing valuables, and being informed about local events. It's also critical to take health precautions, such as wearing bug repellent to prevent mosquito-borne illnesses.

Q: What is the language spoken in Belize?

A: English is Belize's official language, making it simpler for English-speaking visitors to communicate. Spanish is also widely spoken, especially in the northern and western regions. Furthermore, Kriol (Belizean Creole) is widely spoken, and several indigenous languages are spoken in certain areas.

Q: What are some of the must-try dishes in Belize?

A: Belizean cuisine incorporates Creole, Mestizo, Garifuna, and Maya influences. Rice and beans with stewed chicken, fry jacks (deep-fried flatbread), ceviche (lime-marinated seafood), and hudut (a Garifuna dish of mashed plantains and fish in coconut broth) are all must-tries.

Q: Can I drink tap water in Belize?

A: While tap water in certain parts of Belize is safe to drink, it is generally recommended to drink bottled or filtered water, especially in more remote areas. Most hotels and restaurants provide bottled water.

Q: What are the transportation options inside Belize?

A: Belize offers a variety of transportation options, including domestic flights, buses, water taxis, and car rentals. The country's small size makes it easy to travel between locations. Public transportation is reasonable, but renting a car provides more flexibility.

Q: Are there any cultural customs to be mindful of?

A: Belizeans are generally friendly and respectful. It is customary to greet someone with a handshake and formal titles (Mr., Mrs., Miss) followed by their last name. Tipping is expected at restaurants and for services, with 10-15% being the norm.

Q: Can I use my cellphone in Belize?

A: International roaming is available, although it may be expensive. Purchasing a local SIM card or eSIM is a low-cost option for data and calls. Digi and Smart are two of the country's major mobile networks, and both offer adequate coverage.

Printed in Great Britain
by Amazon